SPLINTERS

SPLINTERS

A Memoir

Rex Hudler

For information:
Rex Hudler
1100 Irvine Blvd. #647
Tustin, CA 92780
or RexHudler.com

Library of Congress Cataloging-in-Publication Data has been applied
for.

ISBN: 978-0-615-21615-7

DEDICATION

I want to dedicate this book to my wife, Jennifer, who continues to love and support me and our children. I didn't think it was possible to love you more than when I first married you, but I do! Now I understand God's gift of unity in marriage. To my children who were made from that love, you are so precious to me. There is no love greater than the love of God and the love He gives us for one another.

CONTENTS

CONTENTS

PREFACE

by Joe Torre

I took over as manager of the St. Louis Cardinals in 1990 when Rex was on the club. The first thing I could see in Rex Hudler was that he had plenty of energy. If I ever needed a player to volunteer to catch, Rex would raise his hand—he was one of those utility guys that every ball club needs for a shot of energy. We were playing the Cubs at Wrigley Field and the Cubs' manager pulled a lefty starter and brought in a righty reliever, and with that Rex turned around to look at me. And I said, "What are you looking at me for? Go up and hit!" Later on, I asked him why he was looking at me and he said, "Whitey (Herzog) used to pinch hit for me in all those situations." I told him, "Don't give me that information because Whitey is a great baseball man; don't tell me something I don't want to know."

It's tough to be close to a player, but Rex was about as open and as honest as any guy I've managed. He used to make light of his ability, but when he played between the lines he was as good a teammate as you could find. He was very respectful and I admired his honesty. As a manager you always appreciate guys who go out there and give you every ounce of energy they have—and that's what Rex was all about. He was about as real as they come. Ability-wise, he swung the bat hard and ran hard and ran into walls.

I remember when he started broadcasting for the Angels, I'd watch him and then I'd critique him. Based on my experience as a broadcaster I decided to give him some instruction and he accepted it, and he continued to be just Rex anyway—a colorful guy. He sort of reminds me of Mike Shannon of the St. Louis Cardinals, that hometown guy who people relate to and enjoy.

Rex is also a very spiritual person and the language in the clubhouse and in the manager's office isn't always pristine. Rex understood it went with the territory. And he sort of put it into perspective; he allowed you to be who you were and certainly knowing that he didn't use those words, Rex never looked down at anybody who used them as punch lines.

When I was doing the Yankees pre-game media meetings, Rex would show up late and I'd chase him out. He'd always take it the way I meant it—it was about having fun. And I continue to give him a hard time—it's so easy to love this guy.

There was one time my wife had a dream and when she woke up she said: "Play Rex Hudler today!" I did play him and we won the game. I may have mentioned this to Rex once, but I never wanted to give him that kind of ammunition.

Rex is deeply devoted to his religion. The good Lord knows that Rex and Jennifer are people who can raise a child with Down syndrome with love and compassion. What other people view as heartache, Rex welcomes as a blessing from God.

— **Joe Torre**
Dodger Stadium
April 2008

Author's Intro to "Splinters"

Some people wonder about me a little bit; they want to know where I get my enthusiasm, passion and energy. They want to know how I handle the ups and downs - - what I call the "splinters" in my life, and stay so positive. I want to be as transparent as possible and I also want to express where I'm coming from and what I'm really all about. How I handle everyday life and the source of my passion and enthusiasm comes from my faith, my God, and my love for life and the love of other people. So, I decided that this is a good time to share some of my life experiences in the hope that it can be an inspiration to others.

THE GUIDING LIGHT

Most people think of me as a lighthearted person and that's true, but there's a serious side to my life that's at the core of everything I do. My faith in Jesus Christ is a big part of my experience on and off the baseball field and in and out of the broadcast booth.

I was nine years old when Christ came into my life. My dad, Marlyn Hudler, worked for Equitable Life Insurance at the time and they were talking about transferring him from our home in Fresno, California to Alaska. Our whole family was going to move far away from everything and everyone I had ever known.

This was a tough time and so I sought the help of Bob Ennen, my Sunday school teacher, a handyman who drove a little yellow truck and had a big heart. He'd pick me up with my buddies and take us to church on Sundays. During the week he would often knock on my window before the sun came up to make sure I was ready for Bible study that was held at a local restaurant.

One day after church we were sitting in his truck and I confided in him that I was worried about moving to Alaska. I didn't want to leave Fresno. Bob told me I needed to put my faith in the Lord—the one who drives the car—and the

Lord is Jesus Christ. If I would trust in Him to guide my life, then He would allow great things to happen.

Bob told me that it was okay for me to submit my request to Christ and that if I prayed on these choices in my life, He would allow for the desires of my heart to come true.

The problem was that I didn't feel like I had a personal relationship with Christ. Bob told me to confess my sins, admit that I'm a sinner, and believe that He rose from the dead to die for our sins. Christ has life and He lives eternally and sends the Holy Spirit into our lives. Bob gave me this simple prayer to say to the Lord and I confessed my sins:

"I'm a sinner Lord; I need your help. Can you please help guide my life?"

And that's the moment I opened my heart to Christ. It wasn't like a big tidal wave that came flowing in. It wasn't like I was shocked and blown away. It wasn't like lights were flashing and fireworks went off. But I felt a security in my life. Once you're in the Kingdom, you're in for good. I prayed that God's will be done and that our family would never have to leave Fresno. Now I know that prayers are not always answered in the way we wish, but my dad's transfer never came through.

I believe everything that has touched my life since that day in Fresno has come from God. I have the late Bob Ennen to thank for sharing his faith. His leadership and counsel helped me learn to allow God to drive my car through good times and bad.

SPLINTERS

WHERE IT ALL BEGAN

I was born to Ann and Jack Mobley in Tempe, Arizona, but my family moved to Fresno when I was very young. My biological father, Jack Mobley, was in the steel business in Fresno, a working class town with working class values.

My early recollections of Fresno and my father, Jack, were of trips to our local lakes to race boats and traveling to the edge of town to enjoy the drag-racing scene. It was so nice to be with my dad in the beautiful hills of the Central San Joaquin Valley. I think this was the very beginning of my love of driving through the countryside and that feeling of freedom.

We used to drive our car to the same foothills and shoot my father's .22 pistol at cans and bottles. It was a lot of fun. We would laugh and joke with one another and share quality time that I won't forget.

I was the middle son of three boys. My brother Richard was 16 months older and Vincent was three years younger. We were all strong-willed but we stuck together. We fought hard for each other and with each other. We were a handful for my mom, Ann, and my father.

I remember being out at Millerton Lake just northeast of Fresno one afternoon. We were having a great time when my little brother, Vincent, was knocked over by a wave and went under the water. My father came out of nowhere to swoop in and save him from drowning. Nice catch! That's what fathers are supposed to do, protect their children, right?

We loved our father so much and he protected us, but there was trouble at home. We really didn't understand how bad it was. Some memories during that time are more painful than others and some are more joyful. While I've not shared all of my memories, I believe some are very important, yet hard to re-live. In no way do I mean any disrespect to my mother, my father, or any other family members.

One of the most painful and disturbing memories that really had an impact on my life was when my brothers and I were awakened by a scream late one night. We ran to the kitchen and my mom was lying on the floor. Jack had smoked her in the eye with a punch. She called the police, and a few days later she told us that my father was moving out and they were going to get a divorce. Although Jack later regretted it, he drank a lot in those days.

My broken family was the first splinter in what was to become a long list of challenges that God has asked me to overcome—and with His help, a lot of prayer, and forgiveness, I've been able to do it.

These were tough times for our family. My mom worked all day as a medical assistant and we would stay with a babysitter until about 6:00 PM when she got home. She was a brave, hard-working woman and she did everything possible to take good care of us boys. No matter how long or how hard she worked, she always prepared a hot, home-cooked meal at night.

About a year after the divorce my mom met someone new, a great guy by the name of Marlyn Hudler. He'd play ball with us and we'd watch *Voyage to the Bottom of the Sea* on TV. He was a kind-hearted person and a good companion, fun to be with.

My mom asked us, "Do you boys want a dad? He wants to marry me but do you guys want me to marry him? Do you like him?"

And we said, "Oh, mom, he'd make a great daddy—we love him!"

She married him and we moved from the Hoover District to the Bullard District of North Fresno. I was 8 years old and it was a new start for our family.

We still saw my father, Jack, every once in a while. He would come on visitations and pick us up to go to the movies or to the park. But there were other times when we'd be waiting out on the porch for him and he would never show up. My mom would stick her head out the front door and say, "Boys, I don't think your daddy is coming today." We'd be waiting out there for two or three hours and he didn't even call to say he wasn't coming. "What could possibly be more important than spending time with his sons?" I thought to myself.

I was young but I knew that something was not quite

right. I never got angry at him because the next time he'd show up and it was like nothing had ever happened. It was like having two fathers and we were trying to make the best of the situation.

Then one day after a visitation, he dropped us off in the driveway of our home. His girlfriend came forward and told me and my brothers that we should say a final goodbye and hug our father because we were never going to see him again. And I'm thinking to myself, "Who are you to tell me I'm not going to see my father anymore?"

I was angry. But we hugged him goodbye, went inside the house and my mom and my new dad, Marlyn Hudler, were waiting to talk to us. That was the old way of parental communication where you basically didn't tell your kids what was going on. I was crying by now. It was so painful because I was being told I'd never see my father again.

My mom said that Marlyn was going to adopt us; we would take the name of Hudler as our own name. My father, Jack Mobley, was going to start a new family and wanted to stay out of our way and not interfere so we could start our new family. The court papers were signed that changed my name from Rex Mobley to Rex Hudler and that's when I believe my competitive spirit was ignited. I had to overcome this trauma, this splinter, and make the best of the situation. We had no control over it anyway.

As difficult as it was, life went on with my new family. Marlyn played ball with my brothers and me in the backyard almost everyday. I loved to play ball and he encouraged me to focus on what I was good at and what made me happy. My dad taught me a lesson that has stayed with me to this day. He said, "Rex, never quit! There's no such word as quit or can't!"

I started playing Little League the year after Marlyn adopted me. I remember going to the baseball diamond to try out with a number pinned on the back of my uniform. That's when the competitive juices really started flowing. I was a little nervous but I couldn't wait to show off my talents because I thought I could hit, throw and run better than any of the other kids my age. There were a lot of Little League coaches there that day who must have thought so too. They were trying to get me to skip the minors and move right up to the majors.

My dad was against my jumping up to the majors because those kids were three years older than me. He told those major league coaches not to draft me. So we went back to the house after Little League tryouts and we did our usual routine of yard work—my dad loved doing yard work—which meant cutting the grass and pulling up weeds.

We were working on the sprinkler system one Saturday afternoon, taking in the blazing Fresno heat, when three men knocked on the front door asking to talk to my dad. "Mr. Hudler, we just came to tell you we drafted your son to play in the majors this season in Little League."

My dad was livid. "Did you guys not hear me correctly

when I told you I wouldn't let him play in the majors? I don't care if you drafted him or not because I'm not letting him play in the majors this year!" And - - he didn't.

So I was only nine years old and I had coaches fighting and battling over me! I was beginning to think I must be a pretty good baseball player if these guys wanted me to play on their team so badly. I have always thrived on positive feedback and I loved being the center of attention.

That's one reason I was so excited when my dad entered me in a Phillips 66 pitch, hit and throw contest—that's where you throw on the bag, throw for distance and hit for distance. I won the local competition in Fresno, went on to win the State Championships in Sacramento, and then traveled to Candlestick Park to qualify for the national competition at the All-Star Game.

I took a flight to San Francisco with my dad (my first airplane ride!) and we stayed at a nice hotel. Phillips 66 paid for everything. I'll never forget how excited I was when we pulled into the parking lot of the stadium. It was beautiful! We went to watch the San Francisco Giants' Willie McCovey and the Atlanta Braves' Hank Aaron take BP (batting practice). My mom wanted to be the parent who went with me because she and Marlyn had just gotten married. She must have been thinking, "Wow, this guy just joined our family *and* he gets to accompany my son to his first big-league game?"

During the game I was in the right field corner and Willie McCovey hooked a foul ball that smacked a little girl in the head. I remember how awful that looked. That was a nasty thing to see. Ugly splinter!

I can remember every detail of that day. I was wearing a bright red jersey. It was my first big-league game to see live. What a thrill! I'll never forget my dad showing me for the first time how to wear my pants bloused—to have pride in how I wear a baseball uniform. "Baseball players are neat and proper looking," Marlyn said. "If you look good, you'll play good." I looked good, I played good, I competed and won in San Francisco. It was an awesome experience! It was a great trip.

Even though I won in San Francisco, they compared my scores to some kid back east who scored better and he got to go to the All-Star Game instead of me. I wasn't too upset because at least I won a national competition and this gave me a lot of confidence in my athletic ability.

This confidence led me to try other sports. Soccer became my first love and that's where I developed my speed and quick feet that served me well in football and baseball. I played soccer on a club team in 6th, 7th and 8th grade and had a great time playing for Coach Bill Neal. I didn't start playing football until Pop Warner in 9th grade but I learned quickly. I also did a punt-pass-and-kick contest and did well in that, too. Baseball was something I always played competitively, but in the sandlot days in Fresno, it was soccer that came first. I'm glad I played all sports because it helped make me the athlete I am.

Growing up in Fresno where the climate was always great for sports definitely gave me an advantage. The athletic opportunities and competition that Fresno offered made a big difference in my life. Coaches meant a lot to me starting with my Little League coaches - - John Strickland, Robin Baldwin, Vic McIntyre, Ralph Waites, and of course, the best high school coaches I could ever ask for - - Mike Noakes, John Anabo, Jerry Justice, and Dan Robinson. These men and other coaches gave me the foundation I needed to endure 21 years of professional baseball.

Friends and Faith

One of the most important parts of playing sports was the friendships I made along the way. After we moved to a new neighborhood, we also moved to a new church. On our first visit to our new church I was shocked to see Mitch Ribera, one of the toughest and wildest kids on the soccer field. He had the reputation of being a rebel and yet he was right there in church worshipping the Lord. He called me over after church and began talking to me about his faith. Sharing our faith in Christ really gave us a bond in true friendship. About five of the guys on our soccer team went to church together and this group started having Bible study twice a week. This was when Bob Ennen came into my life.

Bob was an older man, a Sunday school teacher at our church, who picked us up at 5:30 a.m. on Tuesdays and Thursdays to learn about the Bible and to learn what it meant to our lives as Christians. I look back on this experience and I'm so grateful to Bob that he cared about us kids enough to make the personal sacrifice to teach us about Christ. He helped us understand the importance of memorizing Scripture so we would have it in our hearts to use when we needed it in life.

When you're a kid you need to know who made the

mountains and how everything in nature was created. I needed a stable foundation at that time in my life. The word of God was something I learned from Bob and I carried it with me in my heart. Being involved in church was a very important part of my life growing up in Fresno and it gave me security.

In junior high and high school I really believed that it was God who allowed me to realize the desires of my heart. I was taught that the top priority in your life is to obey your parents in the Lord. If you obey your parents in the Lord you will have a long life full of blessings. That's from the Bible, book of Ephesians 6:1-3.

Although my two brothers were attending the same church, the message didn't hit home with them like it did with me. They began following the wrong crowds and ditching school. The school principal would call Mom on the phone and she'd start crying. They were making Mom and Dad very unhappy with their choices. My heart was breaking to see Mom in so much pain.

I knew I wasn't perfect, but I was sensitive enough to understand that it was important for me to stay in school and to do my chores at home to help Mom. She was working hard to put herself through school to become a registered nurse. For instance, one of my jobs was to vacuum and rake the shag carpet in our living room. One day I spent hours cleaning it to surprise Mom when she came home from work. I wanted to make her feel good. I wanted to see that happy look on her face. When she walked in and saw the carpet, she hugged me and smiled. Doing my chores and following my mother's work ethic was one of the best ways I could honor God at my age.

My mentor, Bob Ennen, schooled me on verses in the Bible that would continue to guide my life. As I read my Bible, I had all sorts of questions and I often called him up at night—no matter how late—he always answered the phone. Whatever the question, he told me where to look in the Scriptures to find the answer. Bob always said that if I honored the Lord, the Lord would bless me by fulfilling the desires of my heart.

The desire of my heart was always to become a professional athlete, though I didn't know which sport would allow me to achieve this goal. In fifth grade I wrote a paper about wanting to become a professional athlete. I revealed in the paper that recess was my favorite subject.

When we moved into the new school district, I had to establish myself in school and I did that through my dominance in sports. I kicked butt in everything we played during recess. And after being the best athlete in grade school, I quickly proved that I was one of the top athletes in junior high school too. I had to prove that, as the new kid, I could compete at the top level in all the major sports. I made some good friends once the sparring session was over and the testosterone calmed down.

One of these friends was Teddy Papulias who had a big

impact on my life. He was a little guy, half Greek and half Italian, and he had an unbelievable mouth on him. He would talk back; he would sass; and he could back up his words if called upon.

Teddy lived only a couple of blocks from my house and after school we'd play in the park and then go over and grab an after-school snack from his cupboards. His dad would always say, "I got four kids as it is and with you coming in to grab food, I've got five."

Teddy's dad, Pappy, owned a meat market and Teddy and I would clean up the plant at night—that was our summer job. We'd spray the fat off the floor so the meat market would pass inspection the next morning. We had water fights and we'd throw meat at each other. Teddy and I have a lot of fun memories.

I had a lot of fun in junior high school and I wanted to do everything my friends were doing. For me that meant trying out for the 7th grade basketball team. I knew that basketball and soccer were going to conflict with each other, but I still wanted to give it a shot. My parents encouraged me to go out for basketball and I made the team. Only then did I realize that soccer practice and basketball practice were at exactly the same time!

I went to my mom and dad and they laid it on the line. They said, "Son, we let you do this on your own so you'd figure out that it was not going to work. You have to tell your basketball coach that you made a mistake since you had already made a commitment to the soccer team."

I met with the basketball coach and I told him the truth and he shot back, "Son, you should have thought about that before you made me cut those other kids who wanted to play basketball!" After giving me some time to think it over—and I did feel pretty bad about it—he told me to go ahead and play soccer. It was the only thing in my life I ever had to quit!

I'm glad that I did because the soccer team played well enough to compete in the state championships. I was an attacking center-forward. Soccer developed my speed so my teammates would push the ball to me and I'd outrun everyone and score. I suffered a couple of concussions because I played hard and fast. I would dive to head the ball and end up getting kicked in the head.

I had no idea where my speed and athletic ability was going to take me. My social group expanded as I continued to excel in sports and so did my church group. I learned more about the Bible. I came to understand how to treat people and how to live my life. I was a good kid because I believed in the importance of school and church. That's how my friends felt too.

We were the top athletes in school, but we weren't walking around campus trying to impress people. There were a bunch of bullies and tough guys in our school, but the athletes were not the tough guys. The tough guys in school learned to respect me because they knew my heart was Christ-conditioned. I loved people, respected everyone, and was very humble and I think people could feel that about me.

Things were going well for me in school and it helped that I was now more involved at Northwest Baptist Church on Sundays and Wednesday nights. The leader of the congregation was a great preacher named Bufe Karraker, a roughneck type of guy. Mitch Ribera and Teddy Papulias were there with me in church twice a week and our friendship continued to grow stronger. We have remained lifelong friends. My foundation in Christ was the constant that got me through the good times and the tough times in junior high school—and for the rest of my life.

THE ROAD TO
NOTRE DAME

My junior high years sped by and then I went off to Bullard High School which had one of the best athletic programs in Fresno. It was the powerhouse in "The Valley." Mike Noakes was the legendary Bullard baseball coach. When I made the varsity team as a sophomore, (I was the only sophomore to make the team), it made me feel good. Since I wasn't getting a chance to play much on the varsity team, I opted for JV instead. I asked Coach Noakes if I could go down and play on the JV team. He said that I could and it paid off for me. Baseball is a sport you have to play to get better!

I also played JV football my sophomore year as a wide receiver and outside linebacker. I loved hitting people on the field. We talked my buddy Nick Papagni, into playing on the team too. In my junior and senior years I started doing really well at football once Nick took over as the quarterback. We were an incredible weapon because we had played every sport imaginable together in the neighborhood park as kids. We had a fake-out play called the "out-and-up", where I'd decoy the defensive back and run 60 yards down the field to score a touchdown. He had a golden arm and could throw

70 yards on the line—tremendous arm!

I was still playing soccer but my parents said, "Hey, son, you're getting letters from colleges and you're playing three sports. You're good at all three but why don't you eliminate one of them so you can concentrate on two sports and be great in one or two instead of being good in three."

That was good advice! I decided to eliminate soccer because there was no future in it for me and I was looking ahead to my ultimate goal of becoming a professional athlete. I focused on football and baseball and in my senior year, I had an outstanding football season. We played in the Valley Championship against Bakersfield West and I caught 22 passes in that game! Even though I was being triple-teamed, I was able to make 10-yard catches because they didn't want me to beat them deep.

I had lots of colleges trying to recruit me and I made campus visits to Arizona State, Cal Berkeley, Michigan State, Notre Dame and Fresno State. When I visited Michigan State, Kirk Gibson came to meet me at the airport. There was 13 feet of snow on the ground and my ears almost froze off. I didn't know anything about their star athlete, Kirk Gibson. I was just a green, 17-year-old kid from Fresno, but Gibson was nice enough to show me around for three days. MSU had an indoor 440 track and Gibson was running with other football players and lapping them! I was thinking this guy was some kind of a freak of nature. Then the next day we played pick-up basketball and he was jamming the balls in backhanded from underneath the basket.

I decided to ask Gibson to show me around the baseball program and he told me, "Baseball is a sissy sport. It's for girls." Okay, I have to admit I was surprised, but I did convince someone else to give me a look at the indoor baseball complex and I was impressed. Later on, when I got to the big leagues in '84, I saw Gibson at Tiger Stadium. I walked up to him at the batting cage in my #56 Yankees uniform and asked in a very timid voice, "Hey, Kirk, remember me? I thought you said baseball was a sissy sport." He said, "Yeah, I remember you, little punk! What are you—the bat boy?" I kind of knew his personality from when he showed me around at Michigan State; surly, confident, and cocky - - but I was blown away that he remembered me at all!

I also met with Darryl Rogers, the MSU football coach, who was in awe that I actually caught 22 passes in one game in high school. "Son, we have wide receivers at MSU who have been here three or four years and have not caught that many passes in their entire career!" My 22-catch game was a good selling point. It was a state record at the time.

Next stop on the recruiting tour was Notre Dame. When it comes to tradition, it's hard to compete with The Fighting Irish. Dan Devine was the coach and he called me into his office and sat down at his desk with my file in front of him. "Son, I'm reading off your stats and we have a scholarship here for you at Notre Dame."

I was in shock! I was being offered a football scholarship at what I considered the top program in the country—they were coming off a national championship in '77. I grew up in Fresno watching the Sunday morning replay of Notre Dame Football games narrated by Lindsey Nelson. I would wake up early Sunday mornings, turn the volume way down so I wouldn't wake my parents, and maybe I wouldn't even go to church that day so I could watch the entire game from start to finish. Now, here I sat in Dan Devine's office being offered a scholarship!! Pinch me!!

I told Mr. Devine that I would talk to my parents. My mom and dad were excited for me and were 100% in favor of my going to Notre Dame to play football. The problem was that I'd taken the SAT exam the day after I caught 22 passes. I had a lot of trouble focusing on the test because I was pretty beat up and so I bombed it—I think I scored something like 600 combined.

Mr. Devine called me up and asked me to take the test again. I did and I scored about 900. That score was not nearly good enough for Notre Dame so Coach Devine asked me to take it again and the third time was the charm.

When I signed the scholarship to Notre Dame, it was big news in Fresno. "Hudler Inks Irish Pact!" "Hud Signs With The Fighting Irish!" That was huge. I'd walk through the halls at school and people would point at me because I was the kid who was going to Notre Dame. But I didn't let it go to my head. My prayers were, "God, you put me where you want me!" Like always, He is faithful!

After I made all my recruiting trips to visit colleges, my mom came to me and confided that after 10 years of marriage, she was not happy with my dad, Marlyn Hudler, and she wanted to get a divorce. I asked her to wait one more year so I could get through high school. I told her I couldn't handle another divorce. That was so selfish of me. We all knew they were not happy together, but she decided to wait.

My mom and dad later divorced but Marlyn still played a big part in our lives. Several years after my mom completed nursing school, she married Dan "The Man" Mueller.

CHOICES & BLESSINGS

With the Notre Dame scholarship signed, sealed and delivered, I was playing baseball just for fun in my senior year and having a great season. The baseball scouts started calling on me and guys in dark glasses and clipboards were coming to the games. I was showing off for them. I would say to myself, "You like that? Well, watch this next play." I loved the attention and that still hasn't changed to this day.

I won the Triple Crown award (most home runs, RBI's and best batting average) that year in a very competitive league in Fresno. The scouts were calling my mom and telling her I could be a No. 1 draft pick and she was telling them not to waste their time and a draft pick because I was going to Notre Dame to play football. "He has no interest in signing with you, so forget it!"

I came home from school on the day of the June draft and I asked my mom if anyone had drafted me.

"The damned Yankees drafted you!"

"What? The Yankees! In what round did I get drafted?"

"You were their first pick. They said you were the 18th pick in the country."

"Dang Mom, what did you tell 'em?"

"I told them they wasted their pick. My son is going to

Notre Dame to catch passes from Joe Montana!" She actually hung up on them!

"Mom, they're a pretty good team—they just won the 1977 World Series."

In the previous college football season the Fighting Irish had been National Champions too. God had given me the choice of a lifetime!

So graduation came around and I had to make a decision about my future. The Yankees had still not called and I was beginning to wonder, but I had to trust my mom's instincts. She was sure they would call again and told me not to worry.

Sure enough, the call came the next day and on the following Thursday I opened the door and in walked Jack Butterfield, the vice-president of the Yankees, and Al Rosen, the team president. I had no idea Al Rosen was a Hall of Fame third baseman for the Cleveland Indians. I was just a 17-year-old punk.

The negotiations were handled by mom and a family friend. We didn't hire an agent because they didn't want to risk losing my college eligibility.

I went off to eat a calzone at Mama Mia's, the local pizza place, and when I came home 40 minutes later, my mom had negotiated a $125,000 bonus to sign with the Yankees. She got my education paid for too. And she said, "I asked for a car for myself but they wouldn't do it!"

"Mom—how could you do that?"

"Well, it was fun. I had a son who was about to walk

away from a full ride with Notre Dame and so I just flat-out asked them for the car. The worst that could happen was they would say no." She always had a good sense of humor and taught me to look on the bright side.

My mom was a huge inspiration. She always taught me to be positive. She would say, "Son, you'll never make it in this world unless you have a positive attitude. You've got to find ways to make a positive out of a negative."

She was telling me all this not knowing that I was about to choose an occupation that is based on negativity. You're doing really well if you fail seven out of 10 times as a hitter. . . .

Ironically, wouldn't ya' know that later my ten year anniversary in the big leagues would be on Mother's Day?!

MEETING
MR. STEINBRENNER

Once I signed with the Yankees I was asked to report to rookie ball in Oneonta, New York. I was told that Mr. George Steinbrenner wanted to meet me and I would stop first in New York City on my way to upstate New York. The Yankees flew me to Kennedy Airport and I hopped in a cab. I made the mistake of telling the taxi driver that it was my first trip to New York City and my first cab ride and how thrilled I was to be away from home for the first time. We pulled up at Yankee Stadium and even though the meter read $15, the cabbie asked me for $35.

"What? But the meter says $15?"

"Yeah, but you've got to get me back to where I came from, Bud!"

So he ripped me off and it was like, "Welcome to New York, Kid."

I was in awe of meeting Mr. Steinbrenner, but when he stepped out of the door of his office, I looked him directly in the eye and shook his hand firmly. I told him sincerely, "It's an honor to meet you. I'm thrilled to be with the organization. I can't wait to help you win another World Championship." He invited me into his office, which had pinstripe carpeting and baseball gloves for couches. He opened the drapes and there was the panorama of Yankee Stadium. "This is my yard. What do you think of it?"

Well, it was beautiful! I was like a kid in a candy shop. We visited for about 30 minutes and all I remember saying was "Yes, sir" and "No, sir." Making a good, first impression was important. I found out later that his children went to Military School. Mr. Steinbrenner liked manners like most people do.

The media took me downstairs and took photos of me in front of Bucky Dent's locker. He was the current shortstop and I was the shortstop of the future. Doug Williams was also in Yankee Stadium that day because he was the first round pick of the Tampa Bay Bucs. They took pictures of the two of us and it was all very exciting. Then it was back to the airport and off to Oneonta for the start of my minor league career.

SETTING THE TABLE IN CLASS A BALL

I was shocked to see the state of the minor league baseball fields. I played on better high school fields than what I found in the New York-Penn League! I also had to adjust to using wooden bats, but it was still baseball and it was still fun. I hustled, stole bases and made the All-Star team as a 17-year-old kid in a league with 22-year-old veteran minor leaguers.

Pete Koury, one of my roommates in Oneonta, was a big, tough, Lebanese kid who looked out for me. There was a bar fight once and he knocked three or four guys away from hitting or punching me. Art Mazmanian, the manager, was a father figure and a really good baseball man. He was strict but I liked it because I was taught to respect my elders and I had no problem with his authority.

I also met Dan Plant, a young catcher from Southern California. He became another of my four roommates. It was like a wild, college dorm situation – a real mess with dishes everywhere! My question always was, "Who's gonna' clean up this up?!" We lived like that for the 3 months of Rookie League in Oneonta.

During my minor league career, I learned how to cook

out of necessity and I picked up a lot of good recipes. My childhood friend, Pete Dalena, played with me in the Yankees organization and he was a really good cook. He made a sandwich that he called "The Base Hit," which had sausages, eggs and some mayo on toasted bread. We'd just kill it before we went to the ballpark. It was primitive! That fit Pete well. His nickname was "Cave Dweller" because he had the uni-brow look.

That November I played in the Fall Instructional League in Bradenton, Florida. We shared the complex with the Pittsburgh Pirates. That was a great experience for me because I was able to meet and compete with so many talented players.

I spent most of the off-season cruising around Fresno in my brand new Datsun 280ZX that I bought with my signing bonus from the Yankees. I worked at Kellner Lumber Company stacking lumber. Between working there and working out at Fresno State with head coach, Bob Bennett, I stayed in shape.

When it was time to say goodbye and head back to work, my mom cried. I took a cross-country drive in my new ride to visit the family all across the USA: Grandma Mobley in Arizona, Grandma and Grandpa Emerson in Texas, Great Granddaddy Cade in East Texas and Grandpa Conger in Louisiana. By the time I rolled into Florida, I was excited to see my good friend Chuck Hernandez, who is now the pitching coach of the Detroit Tigers, and his mom and dad,

Chuck and Erma. They would take care of me and serve me lobster and eggs for breakfast. Chuck and Erma were like my second parents and I truly enjoyed seeing them every year on these cross-country trips to spring training.

I remember when I was a young player, the Yankees had a policy of letting the top pick in the draft sit on the major-league bench during spring training. The organization would invite some of the legends to come to camp and so I had the chance to meet Catfish Hunter, Mickey Rivers, Moose Skowran, Yogi Berra and Whitey Ford. Whitey was the first person to tell me to put sunscreen on my face to protect my skin from peeling. Sunscreen had just come out. A living legend was taking care of me!

Bob Lemon was the manager. Lou Piniella was playing left field one day in spring training and he took a shoe off and threw it over the outfield fence. Then he took his other shoe off and threw it over the fence. He played the rest of the inning without shoes. We were all laughing at him when he came back into the dugout and said like only Lou can say it, "Damn shoes were givin' me blisters—#?/% 'um!" He was so down to earth. Rubbing elbows with those great players really instilled the Yankee tradition in me and the way they went about their jobs showed me the right way to play the game—they were all winners.

BUSH LEAGUE SPLINTERS

I faced three years of struggle in Ft. Lauderdale in the Florida State League. I had to deal with Doug Holmquist, a hard-drinking manager with a negative attitude. I had to deal with the heat, humidity and rain. And I was forced to battle injuries that were keeping me from making any real progress. I busted up my knee and hurt my ankle and speed was the name of my game.

I went to AA ball in Nashville in 1982 and I had a lot of fun and enjoyed moving up the ladder. Conway Twitty, the country-western star, owned the team and I had a chance to meet him and Loretta Lynn. We played in front of big crowds and it started to feel like I had finally arrived in pro ball.

I started switch-hitting that spring and I was having success hitting left-handed for the first time because it allowed me to utilize my speed. When I hit my first lefty slump, Johnnie Oates, the manager, called me into his office and told me that there was a lot of pressure to win so I'd have to give up the experiment and hit right handed.

This was a major setback because I had been struggling against right-handed pitching. I was always off balance and my butt kept flying out. I had good power from the left side of the plate and I discovered that my right eye was my dominant eye and that meant I could actually see the ball better as a lefty. I have no doubt that I could have become an everyday player if I'd stuck with it, but they sent me back to A ball to finish out the year. So I told myself I would make it back to the Big Leagues batting right-handed.

After getting stuck in Ft. Lauderdale for the '83 season for a sixth year of A ball, I was frustrated and ready to quit. I told the Yankees I was going home. But I went back to the minor-league complex and thought, "This is not going to be easy. You're going to grind it out and play your way back. Remember, Hudlers don't quit!" That was a challenging splinter!

I hit well the first two months of the '83 season and I was feeling confident. We were on the road playing in the Tampa area and whenever we were in Tampa, George would put us up at the Bay Harbor Inn and pay for all our meals so we could pocket our meal money. Class act! I decided to ask Stump Merrill, a longtime manager in the New York Yankees system, what he thought of the idea of my writing to Mr. Steinbrenner and asking him for a promotion.

"Not a bad idea, Kid. But he doesn't like long letters so write him a short note." I sat down to write the letter, and with the help of my friend and teammate, Dick Scott, this is what we came up with:

Dear Mr. Steinbrenner:

I have been in A ball for six years now. I'm ready to make progress in the organization. I'm hitting close to .300. I'm ready

for a promotion. I hope you'll consider this request.
      Thank you.
      All my best,
      Rex Hudler

When we got to Tampa, I stopped by the Bay Harbor Inn and took the letter up to Mr. Steinbrenner's office and gave it to his secretary. I was hoping he'd read the letter in a week or so but she said, "I'll take it right in to him—he's here today!"

My butt all of a sudden got tight! I didn't expect him to be there. I went to the ballpark and was warming up and playing catch before the game at Al Lang Stadium. I looked up in the stands and there was Stump Merrill talking to George Steinbrenner. Stump wandered down from the stands with a wad of tobacco in his mouth and called me over. I said, "Well, did he get my letter?" He said, "Kid, he loved the letter!" I had to run to the bathroom to relieve myself!

I got a couple of hits that night while George was watching the game. He was big on watching the games back then and he would make quick decisions based on how well you played that night, good or bad. He was quick to praise and quick to criticize.

We boarded the bus after the game for the endless ride back to Ft. Lauderdale via Alligator Alley. It was a four-hour trip and we didn't have bathrooms on the bus so we had to pull over on the lonely stretch of highway between Naples and Ft. Lauderdale. I was wearing my flip-flops and when I got back on the bus after a pit stop, my ankles were covered in fire ants. I had big-old welts the next morning and I swore I'd never wear flip-flops again on any of those bus trips.

The next morning the phone rang at 8:00 a.m. and it was my manager, Stump Merrill. "Hud, it must have worked—you're going to Columbus!"

I had a talk with myself on the plane to Columbus. "You put pressure on yourself by popping off with the letter; now you better play your ass off and back it up!" And that's just what I did. I hit .300 at AAA the rest of the season and now I was playing second base instead of shortstop.

After I was traded to the Orioles, Mr. Steinbrenner wrote me a wonderful letter about my ability to play the game the right way and to this day, I cherish my friendship with him.

BILLY MARTIN &
YOGI BERRA

In my brief time with the New York Yankees, I was lucky enough to play for Billy Martin, another hustling second baseman who played hard all the time during his career. I was called up from Columbus in '84 and I met the Yankees Major League team in Arlington, Texas, where they were playing the Texas Rangers. I checked into the hotel while the game was being played. I had a message on my phone to come down to the hotel bar and meet Billy.

I put on my best clothes and Gene Michaels, the Yankees executive, met me down in the lobby. He brought me over to the bar to see Billy and there he was, drinking his beer, wearing cowboy boots and jeans. He greeted me with a big smile and I felt like I was hanging out with a friend. "Let me buy you a beer, Kid," he said. "Congratulations on being a Yankee and a big leaguer. I'm looking for great things from you."

I finished my beer and walked down to the other end of the bar and met Mark Letendre, the Yankees assistant to athletic trainer Gene Monahan. Mark called me aside to tell me that Billy saw a lot of himself in the way I played and that we could have the same manager-player relationship that

Billy had with Casey Stengel in the '50s. That was one of the most flattering things I'd ever heard. But he also told me to be careful because the Yankees were watching me.

I'd spent time in spring training in 1984 with Yogi Berra who had asked me to sit down and have a beer with him at the hotel bar. Yogi treated me the same way as Billy—like a real person, a friend you could just drink a beer with and talk baseball. Yogi knew my name! I was flattered!

The next day during infield practice Billy stood behind me watching every groundball hit to me. I could feel the pressure and I was gassed. I was exhausted mentally and physically. Billy wanted me to play shortstop even though at this point, I was mostly playing second base. I was so tired I couldn't hit during BP.

I remember my Uncle Widgeon, from the sticks of East Texas, came to see me play in Arlington. I was not in the lineup my first game. Widgeon and his buddies went down to the Yankee dugout during the game and yelled at Billy, "Hey Billy, put the Hudler kid in—let's go!" I'd never been so embarrassed in my whole life because everyone turned to look at me—the rookie!

In a game later that week at Yankee Stadium, against Seattle, Billy was going to pinch-hit for me and he called me out of the on-deck circle. I put my bat and batting helmet in the rack and sat down on the bench. But the hitter reached base on a walk and Billy pulled me over, "Hey, kid, can you bunt?"

"Where do you want it?"

"Bunt the ball towards the first baseman. Get back in the game and bunt him over."

On the first pitch from Edwin Nunez of Seattle I got a 90 mph fastball on the inside part of the plate—he knew I was up there to bunt. I tried to get my bat angle to bunt to first base and I fouled it right over Billy's head. Billy's yelling at me: "Get the f--#?/% ball down!"

I got the same pitch on 0-1 and fouled it back right over Billy's head again. I looked over at him and he was yelling, "I don't give a s—#?/% where you bunt it—just get the ball down."

I took a step out of the batter's box, it was a 0-2 count, and took a deep breath. I wanted to succeed and to show him I could get the job done. I was expecting another fastball and sure enough I got the same pitch in the same location. I laid down a perfect bunt down the third-base line and beat it out for a base hit. I couldn't have rolled it any better! As I was walking back to the base, the Yankees' dugout was on my left, Martin was looking at me and I spit towards him—take that!—as a gesture. Billy jumped off the bench and pointed at me and was yelling, "Did you see what the kid did to me?" Billy liked it. Now I don't encourage you to spit towards your boss! But he had challenged me to bunt on a 0-2 pitch and I spat at him. He loved that. I was just like him as a player—scrappy!

The moral of this story is that when you are faced with a situation where the pressure is on and it's time to perform, you don't get tight, you relax. You accept the challenge. Now get off the bench! Relax and be confident in the abilities you've been given.

Billy really liked me after that incident. I had passed my initiation with the Yankees. Martin loved my style of play because it reminded him of the way he had hustled with the Yankees.

But Billy was fired after the '85 season and Lou Piniella took over for him. Lou and I never agreed about my hitting style. He wanted me to hit like he did, which was impossible for me. I didn't agree with his approach, so he was very tough on me and that led to my trade to the Orioles. I'm convinced that if Billy Martin had kept his job I would have stayed with the Yankees and gotten an opportunity to play.

Jennifer - The One Who Almost Got Away

I met my wife Jennifer in '84 during my second season with the Columbus Clippers. Jennifer was the Director of Music for the Parke Hotel in Columbus, Ohio. We had a season-opening "Meet the Clippers" banquet at the hotel with 500 people attending the event, and one player from the team would sit at each table.

I was wearing a nice suit and sitting at the hotel lounge having a beer with two or three of my buddies before the dinner. Jennifer was working as the DJ at the party in the lounge and I went over to request a Huey Lewis tune. She was wearing a tuxedo and spinning the records—Jennifer is a wonderful musician and singer and was majoring in Opera at Ohio State University.

It was early in the season and I wasn't looking for a girl-friend; I was concentrating on baseball and trying to move up to the majors. Jennifer was hot and she had a pretty smile—that's all I can remember from that first meeting and in no way was I trying to flirt or pick up on her.

I went back to the lounge with my friends after the dinner. At the end of the night I walked out through the lounge and was leaving the hotel and there was Jennifer in a more casual outfit at the front door. I didn't even notice her. She was with two of her friends and she said something to her friends about me. I have no idea what she saw in me— it's hard for me to believe that she was even asking about me.

As I was getting close to leaving the hotel her friends put pressure on her to say something to me, and she said, "Hey!" I'd never had anyone ever try to pick up on me, so I got excited. I asked if I could have her phone number and she said no! I'm wondering, "Why would she call me back if she wasn't going to give me her phone number?" But I got her name and told her I'd call her at the hotel and perhaps we could go out to lunch. She watched me walk out to my car. Maybe she wanted to see what I was driving (I had a nice Turbo Z, a beautiful sports car). Girls like men who drive nice cars, right? Ha! She still had no idea what I did for a living.

About a month later I called her at the hotel and asked her out to lunch. She agreed and over lunch I told her that I was a baseball player for the Columbus Clippers. She told me that she thought baseball players were either womanizers or drunkards and she wasn't impressed. But I told her that all I wanted to do was take her out and have some fun; no worries, nothing serious. It wasn't a proposal or anything like that.

She relaxed and we had a nice lunch. She was sweet and fun to be with and she had a great personality. We went on a couple of dates and went dancing. We had so much fun dancing that there were times when I went to the ballpark the following day with a sore knee. I already had a couple of surgeries on my knee, but we danced so much that my knee would actually swell up.

We dated in '84 while I was in Columbus, and then I got traded to Baltimore in 1985. We dated off and on during this period. I moved to Rochester to play for the Rochester Red Wings, the AAA affiliate of the Orioles, and when we'd play in Columbus, I'd visit Jennifer and we'd go out. We started becoming boyfriend and girlfriend during the three years from '85-'87.

During the '86-'87 seasons I was with the Orioles, and in Miami during spring training. I started praying to God to send me a wife. I wanted to have a life with a partner that would last forever. I wanted my relationship, my marriage, to be for real. I didn't want to ever get a divorce. I prayed; I put pressure on God to help me pick a wife. I prayed constantly for a year.

God lifted Jennifer up in my eyes. I had a few girlfriends, but Jennifer had the qualities I was looking for in a wife. She was beautiful on the outside but she was even more beautiful on the inside. I knew in order to have a successful marriage the woman I married had to be mentally tough to handle a baseball career. And she was tough—let me give you a good example of what I mean by tough.

In the winter of 1986 she was planning to visit me in Fresno and I told her I'd like her to meet my family. I still had a couple of different girlfriends around though. She flew out to Los Angeles and was staying with a friend. She called to say she was ready to fly to Fresno. At the same time one of my other girlfriends showed up unexpectedly in Fresno and I liked her too. I panicked and didn't know what to do so I didn't call Jennifer back.

Jennifer called me before her trip ended and she chewed me out royally. "Just listen. Don't say a word. Who do you think you are? You invited me to come out to California and you didn't even call me back. You say you're a Christian? That's a bunch of crap! Don't ever say that to me again. What gives you the right to treat women like that? I don't want anything to do with you!" She read me the riot act. She buried me. And I deserved it.

My mom had trained me to treat women like queens. Open the doors. Be a gentleman. Be kind. Always put women first.

I was surprised at the tone of the call with Jennifer. But after she hung up on me and said she never wanted to speak with me again, I actually had a smile on my face as I looked down at the receiver of the phone. I liked that tough attitude she showed me. That told me she was strong. She was not afraid and I had it coming to me. She really let me have it. I said to myself, "You won't get away—no way." That's how God told me she was the one!

I let about two or three months go by and left her alone. I was in the Orioles spring training base with my roommate, Tom O'Malley, and we were just about ready to break camp and head back to Rochester. Our first game was in Columbus and I told O'Malley the story about Jennifer. He reassured me that I'd waited long enough and that I should call her at the hotel where she worked—and talk fast.

I took his advice. "Jennifer, please don't hang up on me. This is Rex Hudler and I just want to tell you how sorry I am for what happened. I feel bad about what I did. Please accept my apology. I'm with the Orioles organization now and I would love to see you when the Rochester team comes to Columbus." There was dead silence. And then she admitted, "I've been checking the box scores."

That made me feel good. I went to visit her in Columbus and we pretty much had to start all over again. She was very aloof but she gave me another chance. I knew she was special and I couldn't blow it again! We continued dating through the off season.

That next spring I went to Orioles camp in Miami and I was twice blessed—by getting a locker next to Cal Ripken Jr. and a low number (#1) on my jersey. Al Bumbry and some other great players had worn that number for the Orioles so I was very confident I'd make the team. Sometimes you know you have a better chance if the number on the jersey is low.

After putting on our jerseys one day, I asked Cal for some advice about how to propose to Jennifer and he told me that when he proposed to his wife, he built an illuminated sign in the woods outside of his house that read, "Will you marry me?" He just flipped a switch and the question popped up on the sign!

That was a fun idea, but what was I going to do?

Cal said, "Hud, take her to Key Biscayne, rent a tall ship with sails, don't be afraid to be romantic and then propose to her. If she says no, throw her overboard!"

I decided to rent a boat down at Key Biscayne and follow his advice—except for the part about throwing Jennifer into the Bay. I chartered "The Spirit of Miami," a beautiful tall ship. I bought two engagement rings to offer her a choice with two different looks and, of course, I brought along a bottle of champagne. We sailed out into the Bay at sunset and the captain spied on us while I was getting ready to propose.

I asked her to marry me and there was silence. It's the kind of silence that makes a man sweat. What seemed like 20 minutes was really about 20 seconds. It was a long silence. Would I have to throw her overboard? What was I going to do if she said no? I felt a cold sweat forming on my forehead.

Finally, she said she'd marry me but she wanted to wait another year. I told her that was fine, she was worth waiting for. I was just so relieved that she said yes! That's all that mattered to me.

I finished the '87 season with a stress fracture in my shin so I couldn't play for the Orioles—in Baltimore or in Rochester. I was on the DL (disabled list) for a long time and the doctor prescribed no running for four months. Wow, that was a tough splinter! I missed the last three months of the season. I went home to Fresno, California, and I asked

Jennifer if she'd come home and hang out with me during the off-season. I wanted her to get to know my family.

I was working that off-season for my father, Jack's, steel business where they fabricated steel for construction projects. I was a purchasing agent and I wasn't very good at it. I was dealing with the stress fracture and I didn't have a team to play for the next year because the Orioles had cut me loose.

It was a really tough time in my life. I was unsure about myself. But at the heart of it was that I didn't feel comfortable about Jennifer staying with me in the apartment we rented. God was not happy with me because all the things around me were going bad. My dad's company was struggling to make a profit and it went under that year. He had to close it down. I was depressed about that and I didn't know what to do about my brother who was having some problems. It was a horrible time.

I talked to Mitch Ribera, one of my best friends, and he told me that I was not honoring God because I was living with Jennifer before we were married. "I don't think God is pleased with what you're doing with your life, Hud." Mitch was not afraid to say what I needed to hear! I believe we all need accountability.

I felt the same way and I told Jennifer, "Honey, I want our marriage to last a lifetime and I want God to honor our marriage. In order for God to honor our marriage we can't live with each other until we get married. We need to honor Him. We need to make that sacrifice for 5-6 months during the upcoming baseball season. I don't know where I'm going to play but I feel like I'm going to play for some big league team. Let's wait until October 22 (the date of our marriage) and we'll be bonded in marriage. But until then, let's honor God and He'll bless our lives. It's worth it!" She agreed. We decided to do what we felt in our hearts was right to do.

EARL WEAVER

The time I spent in the Orioles organization was frustrating, but one of the highlights was playing for Earl Weaver and the Ripken family. The Earl Weaver legend lives up to the hype. I could not believe how much he cursed and he was always going at it with the umpires over balls and strikes. Earl and Billy Martin were a lot alike—tough, old school guys with quick tempers.

One of Earl's many rules was that the young players could not leave the bench to go down to the clubhouse during a game. A young player was supposed to be on the bench watching, learning something to build on. I broke the rule and I was hanging out down in the O's clubhouse with Jimmy Tyler, the longtime clubhouse man for the Orioles. In fact, he's still taking good care of their clubhouse.

Something happened in the game that pissed Earl off and before Jimmy and I knew it he was coming down the tunnel to the clubhouse, cursing and yelling. I looked at Jimmy Tyler. His eyes became as round as saucers and he took off and ran out of the clubhouse. If Jimmy Tyler was running away, what should I do? I didn't want Earl to catch me and so I hid in a locker and pulled jerseys over my body to stay out of sight. Thank God he didn't see me or I probably would have been sent packing to Rochester.

I came out of the locker when it was safe and snuck back to the bench. I never went down to the clubhouse during the game again after that incident. Earl was a Commander in Chief type of leader and he scared me to death.

The Ripken trio of Cal Sr., Jr., and Billy was worth every penny! I learned about serious baseball between the lines from Cal Sr. who was a great teacher and enforcer. His boys had the same competitive nature and great sense of humor! They were a class act and still are.

EYE OF THE TIGER

I met my agent, Arn Tellem, through Bobby Meachum, the New York Yankees third base coach when I was there in 1984. Steve Greenberg was Meach's agent and Arn was Greenberg's assistant. Greenberg ended up working for the owners and Arn took over his business. Since it would have been a conflict of interest for Greenberg to represent the owners and the players, Arn got his chance to run the business full time. I met with Arn in Columbus and I decided to sign with him and I've never had another agent. I love Arn. He's married to Nancy and has 3 great boys. He's a gentleman—unless you cross him!

I got my release from the Orioles after the 1987 season and was a free agent that winter. My off-season training was going great and I told Arn that all I wanted was an invitation to a big league spring training camp. Arn told me, "Hud, I'll get you a big league invitation to spring training in '88. But you have to do the rest."

I was in great shape. I was lifting weights but I wasn't running because of my stress fracture and speed was the name of my game. The Baltimore Orioles doctor had told me I couldn't do any running for four months. I saw another doctor in Fresno to get a second opinion. "Hey Doc, spring training is only a month away. I have to start doing some running, man!"

The doctor started training me in the water—running underwater. I worked out with weights and then did my swimming. I started taking groundballs and I was able to catch up speed-wise in a month.

Arn got me a job with the Montreal Expos. Gary Hughes, now a scout for the Chicago Cubs, had been responsible for the Yankees making me their first round draft pick. Hughes kept his eye on me while I was with the Orioles and when Bob Melvin, the GM, let me go, I became a minor-league free agent. Gary gave me a second chance with the Expos. Gary is like a father to me!

I went to camp with the Expos and I was flying around the bases barely touching the ground! I was really fast that spring. I was in the best shape of my life, but I was not in baseball shape and my timing was off for hitting. During the first week of camp, after two days of just taking batting practice, you start playing against your own teammates in intrasquad games. On the Expos team I was facing guys like Randy Johnson, Sergio Valdez, John Dopson, and Brian Holman — all hard-throwing, blue-chip pitchers with great stuff. The pitchers were way ahead of the hitters early in the spring. After the second week of camp, Buck Rodgers, the Expos manager, called me into the office to tell me he was sending me out to the minor-league complex. According to his assessment of my skills, "You can't hit. You can't field.

The only thing you can do is run and you can't steal first base in this league. You haven't shown me a thing."

I was looking back at him with a big smile. I'd been through a lot of things in my life in the past six months. I knew I was getting married. I believed it was going to be a big year for me. And I knew I wasn't ready with my baseball skills but that given time everything would be okay. "Well, kid, what do you have to say for yourself?"

"Hey, Buck, what I am supposed to say? Let me tell you something. I missed almost all of last season. I'm not in great baseball shape, but I'm in great physical shape. Send me to your minor leagues—just don't release me! Send me down and in two months, I guarantee you'll have me back on your squad."

He stood up and opened the door—my cue to get out of his office. I was shipped out to the AAA camp; this was the first time in five years that I was sent down this early in the spring. With both the Yankees and the Orioles, I was always one of the last cuts.

Now, I was hanging with 300 guys down on farm and I was thinking, "It's time for "The Eye of the Tiger" to come out in me! It's time to start fighting!" All of a sudden I looked at the clock and I was 28 years old! There was a sense of urgency. My career was slipping away, so it was time do something!

I went down and kicked some ass in the minor league camp. I was very aggressive; I had an intense attitude. My hitting started coming around. When I made an out at first base, I punted my helmet and Ray Guy, the Hall of Fame NFL punter, would have been proud because I kicked that thing 30 yards in the air! I was angry because I was called out at first base.

The next day the Expos held a meeting with all 300 minor league players. "Fellas, we just want to let you know that it's not appropriate to throw or kick any of the equipment in anger. We don't want to see any of that." That told me that there were people in the Expos front office who were watching me.

The next spring training game we played was against Columbus, the Yankees AAA affiliate, and Bob Geren was catching. I came home on a groundball in the infield and I stuck him with a head-first collision at the dish. I can't even remember if I was out or safe but that was the mind-set I had; to win and move up that season.

The next day the Expos brass held another meeting in the minor league camp. "Hey, guys, no crashing into the catchers head-first during spring training. That's how you get hurt—it's only spring training." All my teammates were looking at me and thinking, "Way to go, Hud." But -- I was on a mission all that spring.

The final day of spring training we were going to catch a plane after the morning game. We were playing the Columbus Yankees at Ft. Lauderdale Stadium. George Steinbrenner wanted Tommy John to throw to some hitters as part of his extended spring training program. Bucky Dent was managing Columbus and it was a 9:00 AM game because teams were getting ready to break camp and head north.

I was all over Tommy John. I was always a good "B game" player. I loved the early-morning games with no BP— you just strap it on and go. I'm a morning person so this played to my strengths. I woke up and busted out.

I was the lead-off batter and hit a double. Then I tripled. The next at bat I smoked a line single and stole second. The next hitter, Alonzo Powell, got a base hit to right field and I came running around third base. I had a slightly sore ankle so I slowed down just a little as I reached third base and once I hit third I kept on going. Glenn Sherlock, (now the Arizona Diamondbacks' bullpen coach), was the catcher for the Yankees AAA team that day. Sherlock stood in front of the plate and I dropped my shoulder and stuck him. I cold-cocked him! I went back to my dugout on the third-base side to get some high-fives from my players after scoring the run and they were all stepping out of the dugout with their mouths open to look at the catcher; they weren't even looking at me. Sherlock was down on the ground. He was shaking and having convulsions and they took him out on a stretcher! "Hud, what did you do?" "The guy was in my way. What else could I do?"

They carried Sherlock off in a stretcher and the game resumed. I was playing third base next inning and Bucky Dent came out. (I knew Bucky because he played in the Yankees organization with me.) He was in shock. "What are you trying to do, Hud? This is the getaway day for spring training—what's the matter with you?"

"Bucky, I'm sorry. I wasn't trying to hurt him. It was an accident." The bad part was Sherlock's brother was in the stands with a movie camera and filmed it! Ooooo – ugly!

A couple of the players on that Columbus team were guys I'd come up with and they vouched for me. One of the guys, Pete Dalena, said "Look, this is just the way Hud plays the game. He wasn't trying to hurt the guy."

That's how my season kicked off as I went north to Indianapolis. Otis Nixon was the leadoff hitter and I hit second in the order. This was a comeback year for Otis. He'd had some off-the-field problems and the Expos sent him back to the minors to get his life together. That's when he surfaced with me in AAA.

It was just a flat-out track meet that spring. Right before the Expos minor leaguers broke camp the team timed us in the 60-yard dash and they posted the times. Otis and I were at the top of a list of 300 players with a 6.45 in the 60. I was really proud of my time in the 60 because I'd worked so hard in the off-season with my training.

Otis was a great base stealer. I was never a great base stealer. I had raw speed but I didn't have the technique that Otis had to swipe bases. He was awesome and he was an excellent defensive center fielder for both Montreal and the Atlanta Braves.

So once the season started, the track meet with Otis broke out. We were playing ball and we were having some fun. We wore 'em out! Randy Johnson was our pitcher at Indianapolis. We had the legendary Razor Shines on our team. We were fantastic! Joe Sparks was a fun manager to play for and brought out my best as far as swinging the bat.

Meanwhile, the Expos were struggling. They were in fifth place. Herm Winningham (center field) and Casey Candaele (second base) were the utility guys on the big league club and they were struggling along with the team. Joe Sparks, the manager at Indianapolis, called Otis and me into his office at the same time. This was exactly two months after the season started, and I remember that I had told Buck Rodgers I'd be back to help him in two months. Otis and I had just finished a long road trip. Joe said, "Boys, you guys are going up to Montreal!" I grabbed Otis and we started jumping up and down on the manager's bed. We were jumping up and down like a couple of teenagers. I tackled Otis and I yelled, "This is it! We're getting another chance. Here we go." Joe Sparks was cracking up. "Get out of my room. Take that stuff to another room." Sparkie had a great sense of humor.

Otis and I flew to Montreal, and when we got to the ballpark Buck Rodgers put us both in the lineup with Otis leading off and me batting right behind him in the second spot in the batting order. We just continued the same track meet from Indianapolis. Three weeks later the team had moved up to second place. I was finally getting a chance to play and platooning at second base with Tom Foley.

I ripped off 19 straight stolen bases before they even threw me out. When I would take my lead, I always had an edge—it was my turn now. "I'm going to kick some ass!" My football mentality took over. I was desperate. I was about to get married. I was 28 years old and I had hardly played at the major league level. I knew that if I didn't do it now I'd never make it. I thought to myself, "I'm playing for my future kids—it's not about me anymore."

I had my back up against the wall. I was a number-one pick and all the talk of being a top prospect was bull #?/%. I had to perform. I had to do something. This is a performance-based business.

We were playing the St. Louis Cardinals at Busch Stadium and I looked over at Ozzie Smith as I was running from first base and I said to myself, "I'm going to nail your ass! You're in trouble."

A groundball was hit at Jose Oquendo at second base, who flipped it over to Ozzie at shortstop. Now, Ozzie was doing his straddle the base, jump in the air and throw to first in one smooth, fluid motion. And I did my sit-down, pop-up slide. I came up and he was straddling my shoulder—I had him caught in the middle of his motion. I heard one voice on one side of my head telling me, "You've got to be careful, Hud—that's Ozzie Smith, a future Hall of Famer!" The other voice on the other side of my head told me to "Just slam him!" It was like an angel talking to the devil. I decided to slam him and I put him right on his ear! The crowd at Busch Stadium howled at me. It was like I didn't even know what happened. It was like, "Oh, my gosh, what have I done?"

I ran off the field to a chorus of boos. I'd never heard Busch Stadium like that before. And the umpire called an automatic double play. He told me that I was way out of line.

The next day there was a big color photo in the St. Louis Post-Dispatch of my slide into Ozzie Smith. I was holding him. It was like big-time wrestling and I had him on the ropes. I went to the ballpark that day and I was in the lineup again at second base. I looked over at Ozzie and he walked over to me and said, "Hey, Rex, how are you doing?" Dude, he knew my name! I was like a peacock with my feathers spread out. I was so proud. Ozzie Smith knew my name! Wow! "Hud, you've arrived now," I said to myself. I started to feed off of that incident. That was going to be my "schtick". I was going to play hard, and that's how I'd get recognition.

The Expos flew from St. Louis to Chicago to play the Cubs at Wrigley Field. During our first game, I took my lead off of first base and I was looking at Ryne Sandberg and - - well, those little voices of good and evil came back to me! Sandberg was just a different Hall of Famer in a different city. The ball was hit to Ryne who flipped the ball to Shawon Dunston at shortstop. I came in with a hard slide and knocked him down. The next day I got Sandberg and for good measure, I knocked Dunston down again, too.

During the third game of the series I took my lead and Sandberg was looking over at Dunston and probably thinking, "There's that crazy guy over there! Get me the ball quickly!" I was getting inside their head because of playing hardball. I was fast enough that I could get down to second base and strong enough to deliver a shot because I was 200 pounds. I knew how to play the game.

Damon Berryhill, the Cubs catcher, told me after that season that Dunston ran off the field and came into the Cubs dugout during this series screaming, "Someone has to do something about that crazy man! One of you pitchers has to drill that guy!" The Cubs pitchers didn't buy into this at all. They knew I was just playing the game hardnosed. I didn't come in with my cleats high, trying to hurt anyone. I would just slide into the base to break up the play and knock down whoever was covering.

THE WEDDING AT
SWASEY CHAPEL

Jennifer and I got married in the 1988 off-season at Swasey Chapel in Granville, Ohio in the midst of the beautiful fall foliage. My family came to Ohio and it was a great party. We released balloons instead of throwing rice. Mitch Ribera, my friend and pastor, married us. We had a communion ceremony planned but we had forgotten the silver plate and chalice, the wine and the bread. We didn't realize it until Mitch handed us Doritos on a paper plate! Jennifer and I laughed at the sight of a plate of Doritos for Holy Communion but it worked just as well. He still tells this story to engaged couples in his church today.

During our wedding we got down on our knees and rededicated our lives to Jesus Christ. I admitted to God that I'd been trying to live my own way far too long. I'd been a believer since accepting Jesus when I was nine years old, but I didn't feel like I was letting God be in the driver's seat. Instead, I was driving and running into a lot of dead end roads. I needed to give Him back the control. He can see the future! We can't!

I heard God talk to me in my heart, "Hey, Hud! Where ya' been? I've been here this whole time waiting for you. You saw what you could do by yourself. Nothing. You had a good half-season in the big leagues this year. I'm going to let you have the desires of your heart but you need to use your light and your enthusiasm that I gave you for my Kingdom. I want these people to see your enthusiasm, and that you are genuine and real. I want you to go and share with people."

I felt almost like Moses being sent to the Promised Land . . . the Big Leagues - - wait a minute, wait a minute! Where am I going with this? I'm supposed to be listening to Mitch! I'm getting married right now! Jennifer thinks I'm listening. Did Mitch just ask me to say, "I do"?

All kidding aside, I really did feel that God blessed our lives because of how we honored Him—Jennifer went her way and I went mine until we got married. Then, when we followed God together, I believe He blessed our lives.

BACK WITH BUCK

Next spring I went to camp with the Expos and I was back in Buck Rodgers' office. "Kid, I just want to tell you that you're my utility player this year. I brought Damaso Garcia into camp to platoon with Tom Foley at second base because I needed a Latin leader and I think he's going to help us."

"Hey, wait a minute! It was one year ago that we sat in here and you told me I couldn't hit, I couldn't catch, and all I could do was run and that I wasn't good enough to be your utility player. You need to tell me that I'm a good utility player! I don't want you to settle for some bootleg player."

So I made Buck eat his crow and tell me how good I was! "Kid, you showed me last year that you could play."

"I told you I needed two months to get into shape. And now I'll tell you another thing. That Damaso Garcia is a dog. He's going to quit. He won't play hard for you. He's very temperamental. You've got the wrong guy! I should have that platoon job. I didn't do anything to lose that job." When I left his office, I thanked Buck because this was the first time in my career that I made a major-league team out of spring training. I was happy about that and let my manager know how I felt about it.

Jennifer and I went to Montreal to start our married

life together during the baseball season. The Expos had good players in 1989 and we battled the Mets for first place. The Mets were tough and they had good players too: Darryl Strawberry, Ho Jo (Howard Johnson), Sid Fernandez, Ron Darling and David Cone. I loved going to play the Mets in Shea Stadium because I could feel the heat. We'd go in there and we'd battle. It was awesome! I was in a pennant race in the NL East with New York right where I wanted to be!

I'll never forget that I was at Shea the first time I'd ever experienced a kid cussing me out. This kid was saying words that a sailor wouldn't say. And he was standing next to his mom and dad! The parents were cussing me. The kid was pointing at me and cussing me. I was trippin', but I loved that negative stuff because it made me even tougher. I said to myself, "Wow, welcome to the world!"

It turned out that I was right about Damaso Garcia. He quit after 200 at bats! He left the team and went home—and those were my 200 at bats he took with him! I didn't say anything to Buck Rodgers, but I told him Garcia would quit on the team and that's exactly what he did. I was not a poison slinger so I let the whole thing go. There were times when I got really frustrated! Even though we were struggling, I wasn't getting a chance to play and I was a good player. Sometimes I would stand up in the clubhouse and yell, "Who doesn't want to play today? If you don't want to play why don't you tell that man (Buck Rodgers) and I'll play for you. I'm tired of sitting on the bench; this is getting frustrating. Let's go!" They all knew I could play outfield and infield and so everyone was quiet. They were a little nervous about me and my intensity.

Those Expos teams had lots of good players: Tim Raines and Tim Wallach were the top position guys and we had a terrific pitching staff with starters Bryn Smith, Dennis Martinez, Pascal Perez, Kevin Gross, Mark Langston and Tim Burke was our closer. I had finally arrived and they knew I could play. I wasn't afraid to be myself. I was stealing bases, and in one game I hit a big pinch hit home run off John Franco who was the Cincinnati Reds closer that year. I came up to bat with two runners on base and Buck said, "Kid—go get him!" Tim Wallach called me over to the dugout and he said that when Franco goes to his change-up, his glove gets big. "He's a fanner, Hud." That's a baseball term for opening up the glove when you're going to throw the change-up.

I got in the on-deck circle, got loose, went to the batter's box and saw the glove fan open. I took a change-up off the plate -- ball one. I knew it was coming. They knew I was an aggressive hitter. I swung at a lot of pitches and they tried to get me to swing at balls out of the strike zone. Franco was very good at coaxing hitters to swing at that change-up in the dirt. The glove fanned open again and the pitch was a ball and it was now a 2-0 count. On the third pitch, Franco narrowed his grip so I knew that the fastball was coming. I hit a three-run, pinch-hit dinger in a nationally televised game on CBS! Beautiful!

A big crowd in Montreal saw that blast -- it must have been a giveaway day—ha ha! I circled the bases after the hit and we won the game. I was doing the post-game show on the field and the team was waiting for me when I got into the clubhouse. They were cheering for me! "Hud, way to go!" We had a three-game lead in the division and that win kept us right in the race. We were right at the top of the standings and I wept with joy. Here I was, challenging guys in the clubhouse to enjoy playing the game or I'd take their spot and when I came through, they were genuinely happy for me. It made me feel good.

In the meantime, Jennifer with her opera background, knew how to speak French. She sang the Canadian National Anthem at a home game in flawless French. The Québec crowd cheered. They loved her more than they loved me!

We enjoyed living in Montreal. What a beautiful city! We stayed in Montreal year-round while I played for the Expos. We promoted the team in the off-season and did the winter caravans. We lived in Montreal in the off-seasons between 1988 and '89 then '89 and '90—two winters. We leased a beautiful home and in the winter there was snow on our driveway every morning. I couldn't wait to shovel us out. Jennifer would always say, "Hud, what are you doing? Get a snow blower!" No way! I loved shoveling snow! I wanted her to take a picture of me shoveling out my neighbor's driveway.

It was part of my winter workout. I had fun. The team actually paid us to live in Montreal during the winter. None of the other players would stay there in the winter; all the Americans went home.

I had fans come up to me and ask me to play for their hockey team. They wanted me to be their fighter, their tough guy, their goon! I couldn't skate of course, but they saw the way I played and they figured I'd be a good, tough hockey player. Hockey is the number one sport in Montreal and that's probably one of the reasons why the Expos lost their baseball team.

In 1990, Delino Deshields was coming up to the Expos as a top second-base prospect. That was my third year with the Expos and I made the team without a doubt. Buck Rodgers called me into his office to tell me that he was going to let Delino Deshields get a chance to become the everyday second baseman. Tom Foley and I were going to be the utility guys.

"No problem Buck, I think that's a really good idea. The kid is a good athlete, a switch-hitter, and he can steal bases. But can you please trade me? While I'm in my prime right now (30), I want to go to a team that will give me a chance to play. I can't handle another year of sitting on the bench."

"Hud, stick with me and let's see what this kid can do. Let's see how things go. Fair enough?" It was fair and I stayed with Buck.

In the first game of the year Deshields went 4-4 in his major-league debut. He had two great weeks to open the season. In the third week we headed to Shea Stadium and I was taking groundballs at shortstop during infield practice. Buck walked behind me: "Hey, kid, don't take your laundry out!" That means don't send your laundry out because we're trading you or something is going to happen soon.

The team flew to Houston after the game and the next day we were playing golf on an off day. I told my buddies what Buck had said. They knew something was going on because news travels fast. Baseball players are worse than women when it comes to gossip! The gossip is unbelievable in the game and around it.

My roommate was Mike "Aldo" Aldrete (that was before we went on strike for players to have their own rooms in '94) and after golf we went home to take a nap before going out to dinner. The phone rang and Aldo grabbed the call. "Dave? Ah, hold on." He passed the phone over to me; he was disappointed it wasn't for him. The call was from Dave Dombrowski, the Expos GM.

This was the only team I ever played for where the guys congratulated you if you got traded! Guys wanted out of Canada with its double tax. Dave Dombrowski told me to come up to his room; he had some news for me. I went upstairs and I was trying to read Dombrowski's body language. I'm an expert body language reader and he was a little bit somber. He asked me to wait until Buck came into the room. I was sitting there waiting and when Buck walked into the room, he didn't have a smile on his face either. I was feeling that maybe they were going to send me down to AAA.

They were upset about trading me because they liked me. They didn't want to trade me but Buck knew I wanted out. They told me that I'd been traded to the St. Louis Cardinals. Whitey Herzog, the Cardinals manager, liked me because I had speed. I let them keep talking and then I asked them who they got in return for me. "We got John Costello, a right-handed situational relief pitcher."

"Are you happy with him?"

"He'll be our middle-inning relief specialist and this will give you a chance to go play for a good organization."

"Hey, look, you got me for nothing. I'm happy that you got a player back that you like. I can't thank you enough for the opportunity to play for a National League team and for giving me another chance." We all shook hands and I was walking on air when I left them. I called Jennifer and told her that we were going to the World Series because the Cardinals were picked in 1990 to win the NL pennant.

The word spread around the team that I'd been dealt and I was going to fly out the next morning. That evening all of my teammates came into my room and were slapping me high-fives. They were happy for me but they were bummed that they were not the ones who were getting out of Montreal.

THE WHITE RAT

Finally, with the Cardinals, I had a chance to let people see what kind of player I was. I joined the Cards and became a member of one of the elite teams in major league baseball. The '90 Cardinals were picked by the media to win the NL East, but they had gotten off to a slow start.

When I first became a St. Louis Cardinal, I flew to Los Angeles to meet the team—we were playing the Dodgers. On my first day with them I took fly balls and I took groundballs—the White Rat (Whitey Herzog) said I was going to be their utility guy. I was running around in the outfield, catching balls and working hard, doing my normal routine. When I came in from BP, there was a tall glass of milk in my locker. I'm talking tall! The guys were watching me. I took the glass of milk and I drank it all in one gulp. I put the glass down, took my shoes off, changed my uniform shirt and I didn't even look around to see who was watching me—even though I knew everyone on the team was watching me. John Tudor was the one who had put the milk in my locker as a prank. It was the team's way of telling me to slow down a little bit and to chill out.

Joe Magrane was the starting pitcher for that first game. Magrane and I didn't like each other then but we are great friends now. I had hit three homers off of Joe while I was playing with the Expos. That was when he was the ERA king in the National League. Joe had a rock concert going on and I busted his ass—it was beautiful.

I loved hitting off of southpaws (lefties) —that was my specialty during my career. In five years in the National League and five years in the American League I faced all the top lefty hurlers in baseball: Frank Viola of the Minnesota Twins, Bruce Hurst of the Boston Red Sox, Sid Fernandez of the Mets, John Tudor and Joe Magrane of the Cardinals, Charlie Leibrandt, Tom Glavine and Kent Mercker of the Braves, Fernando Valenzeula of the Dodgers and Kenny Rogers of the Texas Rangers.

Magrane could not get me out and so finally he drilled me—he hit me with a 94-mph fastball right in the thigh! I took first base and I was cussing at him. Pedro Guerrero told me to "Go get him! If you want him, then go get him—there he is." I was pissed! He hit me because I kept wearing him out. I'd hit two home runs off Joe in Montreal and then we went to Busch Stadium and Buck Rogers, the Expos manager, told me I was leading off.

When I went to bed the night before the game I was trying to visualize that first pitch from Magrane. I went to bed thinking I'd see a first-pitch fastball down and in but still in the strike zone because he'd try to get ahead in the count. The first pitch was, in fact, that exact pitch I had been visualizing and I hit the ball off the top of the foul pole for a home run and we were up 1-0 on the first pitch of the game.

That kind of stuff got stuck in his craw and now, here I was joining the Cardinals with him. So, that first day Tom Pagnozzi, the Cards catcher, called me over to the trainer's room at Dodger Stadium. "This guy wants to meet you—it's Joe Magrane." So Magrane and I looked at each other and it had always been tense between us. He stuck out his hand and said, "Just because we're teammates doesn't mean we have to be friends."

I didn't know what to think. What's that all about? Did he want to throw down? I turned around and the whole team was laughing—they had set the whole thing up. It was perfect. That was fun; it took the edge off of being a new guy on the team. They knew they could manipulate me because I was a happy and fun guy. I was gullible. I was an easy target.

I was so proud that I got to play for Whitey Herzog, one of the best managers in baseball. He was so much fun. Whitey was also very good at relaxing his players and I was a very intense guy. I'd get fired up before a game. He'd call me over during pre-game and put his arm around me and tell me a story or two to calm me down.

Once he said, "Kid, did I ever tell you about when I went fishing with "Red Dog" Schoendienst? We were in the boat and we had a cooler in the back of the boat with a couple of cases of beer. Red hooked up a fish and he was battling with it not paying attention to anything else. There was too much weight in the back so the boat flipped over and we all fell in the water. We lost the fish and the ice chest of beer. You should have seen Red. He can't swim and he was searching for a life vest. "

I was cracking up and the time flew right by and before I knew it he was telling me to take the field because our game was ready to begin.

Whitey put me into the lineup one day against the San Francisco Giants at Candlestick Park. The dugouts at Candlestick were like igloos. We had big jackets like the football players wear. But the jackets only came down to my knees and my feet were freezing; I was praying that Whitey wouldn't call on me to pinch run. The only place to get loose was to run down the line at Candlestick. "Kid, get your legs loose because you're coming in the game to pinch run." We're down 1 run, 2 outs, and I started running down the line to loosen up and the crowd was nasty, yelling bad words at me.

Whitey said, "Only go when you get a good jump." I got an okay jump, not a great jump, and I got thrown out stealing by the San Francisco Giants catcher, future Hall of Famer, Gary Carter. We lost the game and when I walked off the field I had to endure watching Carter celebrate like he just won the World Series—he had that "rah, rah" smile and I wanted to get him back!

I was coming out of the shower in the clubhouse and Herzog came up to me. "Hey, kid, you didn't get a good jump, did you?"

The White Rat

"No, Rat, I didn't get a good jump."

"It's okay. Next time you should get a little bigger lead and that will make up for it."

That's how he talked. He didn't make you feel bad. He didn't make it into something really serious. I loved him as a manager. I thought he was great.

I was a dead pull hitter when I joined the Cards. Ozzie Smith would stand with me at home plate during batting practice and say, "Hud, I want you to look at this side of the field over here (to the right of shortstop). You have all that room in right field, right-center, and center field. Hud, you have to wait until the ball gets to you, man; you're way too aggressive. A shortstop in the majors makes that play 10 times out of 10—that hustle makes you look good (on those grounders to the shortstop), but you are nothing but an out."

Whitey Herzog was watching from the batting cage. "Yeah, kid, and by the way, the security guard who sits by the third base dugout has been complaining that you're trying to kill him. Leave the guard alone! Quit pulling the ball!" He would always tell me I could pull a bullet foul. I met Harry Carey for the first time in Chicago near the batting cage too and he said, "Hey, kid, you are the fastest white guy I've ever seen." I was pumped!

Going to Wrigley Field in a Cardinals uniform was a trip because the Cubs and the Cards had one of the biggest rivalries in baseball. The atmosphere was super-charged and I dug it!

My reckless-abandon style of play caught the imagination of the Cardinal fans and Rick Hummel, a great Hall of Fame writer for the St. Louis Post-Dispatch, who was the beat writer following the team. I loved him! The other writer who liked me was Bernie Miklasz, a columnist for the Post-Dispatch, who said that I deserved my own fan club in one of his early articles during my time in St. Louis.

When the Cardinals went to play in San Diego, I was relaxing and looking out the window of the beautiful Marriot Hotel on the Bay. Looking down, I saw people gathering outside the hotel and I wondered what was going on. Then I got a call telling me to get to the ballpark early. When I arrived at Jack Murphy Stadium, there was Red Schoendienst to inform the club that "The Rat" (Whitey Herzog) had decided to retire. He'd had enough and Red was taking over as the interim manager. Whitey Herzog ended up quitting one month after he traded for me! Whitey brought me to St. Louis but now he was gone. It was kind of like losing a father. I felt like I was on my own again so I better keep playing well.

When Red took over, Vince Coleman was out with a leg injury and Red asked me if I could take his place in left field. I had almost no experience as an outfielder except playing center field my junior year in high school. But I had the skills and instincts of a wide receiver and I was a good athlete so I figured I could handle the adjustment. As an infielder you go—1, 2, 3—dive! You don't have to be blessed with range. But in the outfield you have a chance to show your all-out speed. It was like being back on the football field and I couldn't wait for them to hit the ball to me.

I was out in left field in San Diego and Ed Whitson, the Padres pitcher, was batting. We were shading him over towards right-center because pitchers don't usually pull the ball. He hooked a ball off Bob Tewksbury and it was heading down the left-field line when I dove to make the catch just inside fair territory. They had a gravel pit at Jack Murphy Stadium beside the line and I dove right into that gravel pit! When I got up to throw the ball to Ozzie, I had blood all over my knees and elbows. I ripped my uniform and I was pumped! I'd made a 30-yard run to grab the ball and it felt just like catching a football in the end zone and scoring a touchdown. There were 500 Marines from Camp Pendleton sitting in the stands in left field in San Diego and they were cheering me. I looked up and saluted them and they went nuts.

The inning ended and when I went back into our dugout, Todd Worrell and John Tudor applauded me for my catch but were grilling me about saluting the Marines. They were trippin' on me. I wept because I was so excited. I got choked up because I was living my dream; I was playing big league ball, man! And I was contributing to the team. I had arrived! It was a blast entertaining people with all-out hustle!

After the Padres series, the team returned to St. Louis and I kept playing left. In one game I made an over-the-head diving catch and Jack Buck said it was one of the best catches he'd ever seen. I had a chance to show the Cardinals fans my outfield action at Busch Stadium. I was compared to Huckleberry Finn in the local press and I was an immediate fan favorite. It got a little deep.

Jennifer and I bought a home in St. Louis. This was the first home we bought together. We invited all the players over on an off day and had a party. On off days the guys usually go their own way, but when we had our house-warming party, every player on the team was there. And we had a gas! We danced on the patio. They helped me break in the house. At the party, everyone let their hair down and I was accepted. Ozzie and his wife came to the party. Terry Pendleton. Vince Coleman. John Tudor. They all came! We were having so much fun.

My teammates liked me; they could feel me. They knew I was genuine. I fit in! At first they weren't so sure about me because of the way I played the game against them when I was with the Montreal Expos. I had stuck Ozzie with that head-first slide. But once they got to know me as a team-mate, they came to love me. As an opponent, I might hurt you. My game was payback. I had a take-no-prisoners-I'm-going-to-take-names attitude that made me a tough competitor. That was my mentality. But once they got to know me it was all good if they were on my team.

I did take a lot of teasing from my teammates though. I was a very emotional player because I put so much into playing the game all out. I remember the first time I ever got choked up playing baseball. It was when I made my first catch at Yankee Stadium in front of 56,000 people. I made a diving catch against the Orioles my rookie year, heard the roar of 56,000 and I immediately felt a giant knot in my throat.

I got choked up again after I hit a pinch-hit, three-run homer against John Franco and greeted my cheering team-mates outside the dugout. After a close game in Camden Yards, Lee Smith closed the game down by striking out Cal Ripken—and it was a nail-biter; a long game, a battle, and it was so tense that it almost brought tears to my eyes. I again got that familiar, choked-up feeling.

Like most players, I put my heart and soul into the game. Between the lines I would give up everything I had to get my team a win. Some people say there's no crying in baseball, but that's not true. These were tears of joy!

My St. Louis Cardinal days were my glory days. I finally got recognized for my hustle and the way I'd always played the game. I would go to local restaurants with Jennifer, and I was treated like a star. I was a local celebrity. I liked the attention, but after two years of being a celebrity in St. Louis, it kind of wore on me.

In California, people could care less if they see you in public. They leave you alone. But in the Midwest people go up to you to get your autograph and to say hello. I don't mind that, but that's just the differences in people around the country.

Bernie Miklasz wrote an article about me having a fan club and was overwhelmed by thousands of letters from people writing into the St. Louis Post-Dispatch who wanted to join! He even had interest from local politicians and other VIPs. They did a TV special about the outpouring of support for my fan club and Bernie admitted that he had written the column tongue-in-cheek, not really expecting anyone to want to join. He finally had a card made up that said, "Rex Hudler Fan Club." On this little card was a drawing of me doing a head-first slide.

The nickname "Head-First Hudler" was born when Cardinal broadcaster, Mike Shannon, said that I kicked up so much dirt when I dove into a base that I was like a hurricane. My buddy Bob Tewksbury, a pitcher on the Cardinals, was a very good artist. He drew a caricature of me diving head-first into the bag and named it "Head-First Hudler." They put that drawing on my fan club card. T–shirts were made and sold to raise money for the local Children's Hospital. We were taking my popularity and running with it and giving back to the community.

Jack Buck started calling me "Hurricane Hudler" and lifesize posters were made to hand out at the stadium on "Rex Hudler Day". Chris Berman, founder and anchor of ESPN, called me "The Wonder Dog" on TV one night and that nickname has followed me to this day.

I did a radio show once a week on a rock station in St. Louis. I was always good with the media. A local car dealer gave me a brand-new Cadillac to drive around when I was living in St. Louis. I was the 24th or 25th player on the team and yet I felt like a hero. Wearing the "Red Birds on the Bat" logo was such an honor. I always got headlines for anything good that I did for that team and I never took heat for anything.

(Man, I'm not even halfway through the book and I'm already sick of myself! I hope you're not.)

But getting back to me . . . .

JOE TORRE STORY

Joe Torre took over as manager of the Cardinals in 1990 before the All-Star break. (Ironically, he came out of the broadcast booth of the California Angels.) Joe was a great manager. He sat down next to me, asked me what kind of a bat I was using, to make conversation. He liked me. I was playing well when he came over.

In 1992, Jose Oquendo got hurt and they brought up Luis Alicea, (currently the first base coach for Terry Francona in Boston), from the minors to play every day at second base. I went into Joe Torre's office and asked him what's going on. I had been with the Cards for two or three years and they would not give me a chance to play every day. I asked him if he would take out the media guide and check my Montreal numbers when I played on a platoon basis in '88 and '89 and see if those numbers were good enough.

"I have no doubt that you can play every day, Hud, but you're too valuable to me coming off of the bench. You can play seven positions, you can pinch hit, pinch run, and steal a base late in the game. You're too valuable. You're my wild card in a poker hand. I can insert you anywhere and at any time. If you get tired of doing that, Hud, I'll try to move you to another team but I'm just telling you the truth."

I walked out of the office thinking, "I'd take a bullet for Joe Torre. He is beautiful!" I didn't want to be traded. He was honest with me and he made me feel good. I learned something about managing players from that experience. The manager has to love the players and make them feel good. Some managers might want to light a fire under a player but that wasn't necessary with me. I'm a more positive person. I have made some mistakes though.

Once I was asked to sign a Cardinals team baseball on the "sweet spot." I didn't know that the sweet spot is always reserved for the manager's signature so I went ahead and signed it. A little later Rich Hacker, one of the Cardinals coaches, tapped me on the shoulder and said that Joe wanted to see me in his office. My butt got a little tight. Whenever the manager asks to see you it's probably not to give you good news. Joe got right to the point. "Sit down! Let me tell you something. If you ever sign on the sweet spot again I'm going to send you to the minor leagues! You'll be headed to Louisville (the Cards AAA affiliate) on the next flight out!"

"Joe, someone asked me to sign this ball on the sweet spot. I'm sorry."

"Ah, it's okay this time, Hud, but that's my sweet spot!" To this day I won't sign on the sweet spot unless someone asks me to do it.

He was working me. He was keeping me loose and feeling good. I loved Joe. He was so great in dealing with people. One night after a game against the Cubs, he had to deal with a clubhouse fight between Pedro Guerrero and Todd Worrell. Sammy Sosa had just been traded from the White Sox to the Cubs. Sammy and Pedro Guerrero of the Cardinals were good friends. They planned on going out after our game was over. Sosa had hit a home run to beat us on this night and we were not happy.

We were sitting around the clubhouse after the game, enjoying our frosted mugs of Budweiser, but we were in a pretty foul mood after the loss. In walked Sammy Sosa ten minutes after the game had ended and he didn't say a word to anyone. He just sat down in front of Pedro's locker! We all looked over and thought, "What the heck is he doing in here?"

Todd Worrell had just returned from Tommy John surgery (Google it!). He had missed an entire season and had given up the game-winning home run to Sosa so he wasn't in a very good mood.

I was new to the team but very uncomfortable with Sosa hanging around our clubhouse. I asked Ozzie Smith, one of the Cardinals team leaders, to tell Sosa to get out but for some reason Ozzie did not want to get involved. I decided to deal with it myself and walked into the shower area where Guerrero was and said to him, "Pete, your buddy Sosa is out there and something's fixin' to happen unless you tell him to get out." Guerrero told me to kick Sosa out if I was so upset so I called his bluff and went over to Sosa. "Hey, pal, you need to get out of here! You're not welcome here."

Todd Worrell came over and started cursing Sammy—

who at first made no move to leave. I figured I had to go get him when Pete came running out of the shower and started screaming at Worrell. Sammy finally had the good sense to get the heck out of Dodge. Pete decided to charge Worrell, thinking that other players would try to break it up and he would look like some tough guy, but we all took a step back and watched as Todd beat the s--#?/% out of him! He pounded him with body shots like Mike Tyson. Then Worrell stuffed Pete into the locker. All of this happened right in front of the media and it was an all-out brawl. It took six guys to pull Worrell off Pedro and Todd was yelling, "I'll kill him! I'll kill him." Joe was right there!

That same night Joe Torre called Pedro, Todd and me into the trainer's room and sat us down to sort things out. Worrell was so worked up that he started crying. We all apologized to each other and Joe handled it beautifully by saying, "Don't worry about what happened. Stuff like that will happen but please don't do it again with the media hanging around."

The next day Joe called a team meeting to tell us that he loved what he saw because it respected the unwritten rule not to fraternize with players on opposing teams. You don't fraternize because it shows a disregard for the game of baseball and your team. I loved that attitude. Joe respected the game.

I was quoted in The New York Times the following week, "If any opposing player ever steps into the Cardinals clubhouse again, they are fair game." And you know what? I meant it!

IN GOD'S HANDS

The '92 season was a major disappointment for the Cardinals. Torre didn't have a very good team to work with that year. My agent, Arn Tellem, told me that I had an opportunity for a job in Japan! He had sent them a highlight tape of my best plays. They liked the tape and wanted to fly me over to Japan to see what I looked like in person. I decided to go and meet them and see if Japan was in my future.

On the flight over to Japan I prayed to God almost the entire time. "God, if you want Jennifer and I go to Japan and make this team, then allow me to have a good showing. If you don't, then I'll fall on my face over there. It's totally up to you, God."

So I just left it in God's hands. I went over to Japan and had so much fun. I ate the noodles and the sushi. I stayed at a Japanese-style hotel—not a Western hotel, and the bed was very small and so was the bathroom and the toilet. It was interesting and sort of like taking a "miniature" vacation. I loved the food and watched sumo wrestling on TV everyday.

While I was there, I took infield and batting practice and played in intrasquad games. On the last day of the seven-day trip I went to the manager, Katsuya Nomura, one of the most famous Japanese baseball players and the only catcher in the history of organized baseball to catch more than 3,000 games. He thought he was pretty special. He didn't like Americans, but I didn't care about that. I was grateful. I went to him and shook his hand and said, "Skipper, Mr. Nomura, thank you for having me. I loved being in your country for seven days and if I don't make your team, well, thank you for inviting me to Japan. I loved being here! It was awesome. If you don't want me to join your team I'm fine with that. I'll see you."

I went home and was happy to let God guide our course. Arn Tellem called me on Thanksgiving Day (it was the best Thanksgiving we ever had!) and said that the Japanese wanted me to play on their team. "You're going to be a (Yakult) Swallow next year." I was thrilled!

A couple of weeks later I got a call from Japan, and they were telling me that they were going to have to find a new player because the Cardinals were asking $400,000 for me! I wasn't even making that much in annual salary, but they had to buy me off the Cardinals' roster.

I called Mike Jorgensen, the assistant GM with the Cardinals, and asked him to be reasonable. The Cardinals had traded a sore-armed reliever for me who never pitched again. Costello fell on his face with the Expos after the deal and I went on to have a couple of good years as one of the top utility players in baseball. They got me for nothing! So, I said to Mr. Jorgensen, "Jennifer and I really want to go to Japan. You can't stand in my way. Please! I have a chance to play every day finally, and make some money. You need to help me out." I was very respectful and I think Jorgensen appreciated my attitude. I was raised to respect authority. I had the Texas-style good manners of my family.

The Japanese called me the next day and they thanked me because the Cardinals came down to asking $200,000 for me, so the Swallows were willing to sign me to a contract. Jorgensen came through and we had a big signing in Arn's office—Jennifer and I were on Cloud Nine!

I signed for $1 million, which was unheard of for me, and 10 first class round-trip airline tickets. But now what were we going to do with our home in St. Louis? We were going to be gone for nine months. We prayed about it and felt that we should sell the house.

Once we left for Japan, we were thinking that my whole big-league career was over. Five years in the majors was respectable. I thought I was going to finish my career in Japan. I was 32 years old and I figured on making my time in Japan really productive. The Yakult Swallows held spring training in Yuma, Arizona in January and so I had barely a month to sell the house. God assured us there would be no problem and sure enough, the buyer came the next day. It was easy and we made a little bit of money. I believe that God was making it easy because we had prayed and given our lives to Him. He still drives our lives together. I don't always know exactly where He's taking us, but I have faith in Him. That's the whole basis of having faith. If you don't have faith in Him, you can't be blessed by God.

So, I went to Yuma to train for three weeks. Jack Howell was one of my teammates and the only other American on the Swallows. He was a power hitter and a really good guy. He'd already played for Yakult for two seasons and had led the league in home runs.

I had been a utility player for awhile and I needed to brush up on playing second base. The Swallows had hired Rob Picciolo, a long-time major league infielder and current roving infield instructor for the Angels, to work with me on my fielding. I asked Picciolo to help me so he told me to come early to work with him before the regular practice at 7:30 AM. I was taking groundballs while Rob watched and gave me some pointers.

When the Swallows' bus pulled up to the practice field, the Japanese players came over to the fence to watch me take groundballs. They were shocked. Here was an American player arriving early in the morning to polish his defensive skills? That's what the Japanese players do! That's Japanese style. Right then and there they knew they were getting a guy with a good work ethic, who took pride in his job and that goes a long way in Japan.

The rap on American players is they are lazy and don't work. Not me! I had talked to Jack Howell in the off-season about the Swallows and he told me that the Japanese do a lot of extra exercise and a lot of extra work. The key is to do everything they do. I loved it and took pride in how hard I was willing to work to play at my best. I was treated like a king! I went from being a 25th player to being "the man." The Swallows' team photographer even took a picture of me in spring training holding a file and sharpening my cleats. They knew that I was a hardnosed player.

We broke camp in Yuma and got on a plane to fly to Miyazaki, a southern island in Japan where the Swallows had a training base. It was cold there compared with Yuma. After the morning workout we'd go into tents where they had the greatest spread of food I'd ever seen in my professional baseball career. They served us sushi, noodles, soups and all sorts of exotic food I'd never even seen before. The only thing missing was beer, but we drank that at night after the afternoon workout.

"Cactus" Jack Howell wasn't a beer drinker; he was a meat and potatoes guy and a believer. God hand-picked this guy for me to spend time with in Japan—he was the only other American on our team. I carried Jack's bags for him everywhere he went. I carried his duffel bag as a way to show my respect to him as a great player, but it was also my way of telling the Japanese that I didn't have a big ego.

I loved Jack; he was my hero. I made him feel good, too. I didn't want him to get the impression that we were competing against each other. We had fun together during the two months of spring training, February and March. We would run in the outfield for what seemed like hours.

Fighter jets would fly over the spring- training complex

and on the skin of the aircraft was painted the Japanese symbol of the rising sun.

And so, during spring training, we started playing other teams and I matched up against some of the other American players in Japan: Lloyd Moseby, Jessie Barfield, and Matt Winters, a former Yankee who had some pretty good years in Japan. I talked to these guys about how great things were going and they told me, "The coaches will change when the games actually count; just wait and see."

The season started and I hit okay at first, but it was an adjustment period. All their pitchers threw a lot of slop: off-speed stuff, sliders, curves, and forkballs. I had to get adjusted to hitting all the off-speed pitches. If I went 0-4 the coach would come over and ask, "What is wrong with you? Are you okay?"

I was getting picked off of first base because the pitchers were technicians. They were so schooled in fundamentals that it was scary—and it was beautiful. Pitchers in Japan throw 270 innings over the course of a season. They're not afraid to pitch. They are always ready to pitch nine innings. The pitchers in the United States are lucky to make it through six innings. We are finally scouting Japanese players and learning from what they do.

Because I was getting picked off, the head coach called me into his office and told me that they didn't want to me to steal bases. He said they had four guys in the batting order who could hit 30 home runs; it was a power-hitting team and they didn't need me to steal bases. You played each team 28 times and they knew you inside-out. If they got you out a certain way with a particular pitch, they would bury you with that pitch or approach until you adjusted.

We had to study three different pitchers before every game because the identity of the starting pitcher was a secret until game time. That was part of their unusual strategy. They'd banish pitchers to the minor leagues and you'd never see them again. They would pitch guys out of order in the rotation to keep you guessing. It was strange.

Before the game, the managers would exchange lineup cards and no one would know who was pitching until an announcement was made by the PA announcer and then the crowd would go wild. Our manager would fight that strategy by putting the previous night's starting pitcher in right field if he had a platoon situation out there. Then, when he'd bring out the card, he'd make the change in right and put in who he wanted. He'd put the pitcher in any spot where he could pull the guy at the last minute to fool the other manager.

The other team would have binoculars watching our batting practice to see who was warming up before the game, but all the pitchers would warm-up every day to throw the other team off. It was a trick and it was a trip for me.

Some things in Japan kind of got on my nerves. They had a band playing out in left field just like a college football game and every player had his own song. You'd foul off five or six pitches and they would start the song over and over again if you had a long at bat. It drove me crazy. It was like a broken record. The lyrics to my song were: "Get fired up, Rex Hudler. He'll warm and thrill your heart. He plays with all his power and might, Hurricane Hudu-la!" That was my tune. I still know it 14 years later! I would yell across to Jack Howell at third base, "Jack, that song is wearing me out!"

I started using sign language when I was in Japan to be able to communicate because I didn't know Japanese. Jack and I also started our own sign language and body language to form our own secret code during games.

When the Japanese were angry they'd use the "Devil Horns" to get the point across. The coaches used sign language to communicate information and it took time to adjust. But Jack always said, "Hud, you're not going to change their game. You're going to have to get used to that stuff. That's the way it is, man. They are not going to change the game for you."

In one game a guy got brushed back by an inside fastball -- I think it just brushed the top of his uniform -- and he went down like he was shot by an elephant gun. I was like, "What the heck is going on there. The ball didn't even hit him!" The trainer came out of the dugout and they carried him off the field on a stretcher. Five minutes later the same guy came back on the field to a standing ovation. That was the most bush league thing I'd ever seen. He was the short-stop on the other team and I was going to show him what pain was really about.

Japanese players didn't play a physical style of baseball—no one would slide into me at second base when I was making a pivot on a double play and that bothered me. So I slid into that shortstop on a double play and smoked him clean and they carried him off on a stretcher and that time I knew he was really hurt! Tough splinter!

I had to encourage the other Americans like Bobby Rose and Alonzo Powell to knock me down. Those guys did come after me and I loved it. That's the kind of guy I was; I always played with an edge. It kept me on guard.

Two months into the season I was called into the manager's office. He went on and on in Japanese. I asked my interpreter what he was saying and the response was, "You are the reason we are losing. You'd better start playing your game or we're going to send you home." They were trying to scare me.

I shot back, "You have the right man! I'm the guy for the job. Stick with me. Baseball is a marathon, not a sprint!"

"Our scouting report on Leka-sue Hudu-la (the Japanese pronunciation of my name) is a good fielder, good hitter, good runner—when is he coming?" asked the head bench coach. They tried to get inside my head, but I'd been through so much in my career. After 10 years in the minors I'd seen it all, and he was trying to treat me like I was some immature young American.

"I don't want to take your money and go home. I want to play Japanese baseball—kambata kudusai!" I threw the

Japanese fans' term for "fight" at him and turned and walked out of his office.

Guess what? We clinched the league title with three games remaining before the season ended! I had a clause in my contract that I'd make another $80,000 if I hit .300. I was at about .302 and went 1-4 in the clinching game to drop my average to .300.

In Japan the veteran players rested after clinching, but my coach asked me if I wanted to play the following day and I told him, "No, young player today, dozo!" (Dozo means please in Japanese.) He knew that I was batting .300 and he also knew that my incentive bonus kicked in if I finished at or over .300. He looked at me and fired back, "Oh, you chicken heart!" He was hoping I'd play and go 0-4 and lose the money. "Dude, I hit my .300. We clinched the league title. That's what I came here to do." He just wanted to work me a little. We had fun.

We won the seventh game of the Japanese World Series. When we were throwing the manager into the air after the final out (that's how they celebrate in Japan), I wept with joy. My Japanese teammates were coming over to me because I was weeping. I'm an emotional guy and I could not contain my joy. But my teammates could not understand my emotions. They're trained to not show their emotions and so they could not understand me. They kept saying, "Leka-sue, dijoba (it's okay)—we are champions now."

I was just so relieved. What a blessing. Praise God! The joy came from enduring the whole Japanese experience;

getting through the turbulence, ironing my game out, being the man for them, clutching up defensively, and winning it all at the highest level. In the minors I had tons of championship rings but that was not the same. I had endured and we won it all. The crowds were huge, but no one in the US had a clue what I had achieved that year. After all, they didn't care what I did in Japan.

It was amusing and ironic that on the 13-hour flight to Japan, Jennifer and I watched Mr. Baseball with Tom Selleck, a film about an American baseball player in Japan. I saw some humor in it but I was guarded because I was heading into a brand-new situation.

Nine months later, after our team had won the championship, the same exact movie was playing on the flight home! That film was so realistic about what it's like for an American baseball player in Japan. It was right on! I laughed a lot!

We had such a great experience in Japan that the plan was to finish my career there. I wined and dined Jennifer the whole year. It was so much fun playing in Japan that we left our belongings and planned to return for the following season. We won a Championship and I was sixth in the league in batting with a .300 average. I told myself I could be an everyday player.

Two weeks after getting back to the states the Japanese sent me a pink slip and released me. I had a great year but they had a second baseman to replace me the following season. I was really bummed and the money was so good. Their bank paid our bank directly and we never touched my salary. It was too good to be true; not to mention the fight money (bonus money) the owners would pool together for players who had good games.

Once again, I went to my knees. "Lord, is there another door you're going to open for me? I know there is, but please guide me."

"Hud, your work is done in Japan. You went there and smiled. I blessed you to have a good season. I'm going to let you experience what it's like to be a good player back in the majors."

Now my career started all over again. In Japan I learned patience at the plate that I hadn't learned at the major league level. I learned how to hit a breaking ball and the art of self-control. Before I went to Japan, I had been playing only once a week as a utility player and I was always overanxious and I didn't have good at bats. Now I had learned self control over my emotions and that was huge.

I knew that Jennifer and I would miss living in Japan in so many ways. We experienced so much together there and our relationship with each other grew and we trusted God to guide us. We even conceived our daughter, Alyssa, over there—my first child was made in Japan. Ha!

It was no accident that we waited almost 6 years to have our first child; we bonded our relationship before making the commitment to starting a family. I wanted to get to know Jennifer more intimately and take her to every city in the big leagues. I knew once we started our family she wouldn't be able to travel with me as much, but because she had been with me on all the road trips, she'd know the hotels, the cities and the experience of life on the road. I shared my baseball career with Jennifer from the time we got married right through our year in Japan together.

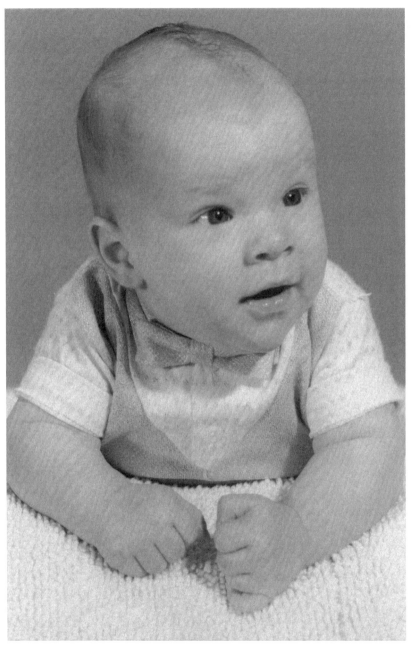

I came out with a "crab" pose. Bring it!

Bob Ennen, my spiritual mentor.

8 years old

Annie, Jack
Me, Vinnie and Richie

Marlyn
Richie, Vinnie and Me

Annie becomes a nurse!

Richie, Vinnie and Me

Headin' to the Phillips 66 Pitch, Hit & Throw
Contest at Candlestick Park

Just a kid with big dreams.

Annie, my #1 fan.

A proud moment with my buddy, Mitch Ribera, aka "The Rug Doctor", before one of our state cup soccer matches in junior high.

My first invite to the Yankees spring training in 1979. I was 18 years old sitting next to then Yankee manager and Hall of Fame Pitcher, Bob Lemon. Wow! I had no idea I would spend most of the next 20 years on the pine collecting splinters! It all started here.

I made it to AAA Columbus, Ohio! I was definitely in the "dig me" stage.

New York, New York! If you can make it there, you can make it anywhere! Frank Sinatra was right.

New York Yankees

GEORGE M. STEINBRENNER III

TAMPA OFFICE
SUITE 890
2502 ROCKY POINT ROAD
TAMPA, FLORIDA 33607
(813) 886-7130

December 27, 1985

Mr. Rex Hudler
503 E. Menlo
Fresno, California 93710

Dear Rex:

I thought I would drop you this personal note following the trade which
is going to be taking you to the Baltimore Orioles. It is probably one
of the most difficult trades I have ever okayed, because as I told Clyde
King, you have always been one of my personal favorites, and I think you
exemplify a great deal of what the Yankees stand for.

By the same token, I do not think it is fair to continue to have you in
a position where you are behind Willie Randolph with no chance for a
starting role in the immediate future, and that is why I agreed to the
trade. I think you are good enough to play regularly--I think that is
what the Baltimore Orioles have in mind--at least I have been lead to
believe that--and I think you will become a fine second baseman for a
very good organization and one of my personal favorites as a manager--Earl
Weaver.

I wish you all the good fortune in the world in your new career, and I
hope you will always remember the Yankees.

Best personal regards,

George M. Steinbrenner, III

GMSIII:deb

When I got this letter from George, I was so proud! I couldn't wait to show the
letter to my mom to let her see what the Boss said about her son! What class Mr.
Steinbrenner showed!

This picture was taken by me on the right. I love my two brothers, Richie and Vinnie. We always have fun when we are together. This was in our younger days!

With the Orioles I played with Hall of Famer, Cal Ripken,
Jr. and Hall of Fame Manager, Earl Weaver.

Engaged at last!

Rex joins the Expos.

In the big leagues you never knew what celebrity would show up for a little action during batting practice! Here is Hall of Fame goal tender for the Montreal Canadiens, Patrick Roy, with me in our younger days back in 1988.

Red Schoendienst made playing for the Cardinals fun.

I could spot a camera a mile away!

Ready for action at the hot corner.

If you ask me, I was always in a bubble during my playing days!

Making our home in whatever city we played in was awesome! Wintertime in St. Louis when I played for the Cards was great! I got to hunt ducks with Hall of Fame 2nd baseman, Red Schoendienst and my hunting buddy, Chuck Reed.

One of our first meals when we got to Japan. Jennifer said, "Is that thing moving?" I said, "Bring it to my lips!" Eating in Japan for 9 months was off the charts delicious!!

Me and "Cactus" Jack Howell, my only American teammate on the Yakult Swallows team in Japan in 1993. We were having dinner with Ikeyama (with the "thumbs up"), our star shortstop and Masa, our interpreter.

I couldn't pass up the photo opportunity with legendary Japanese player,
Sadaharu Oh in 1993.

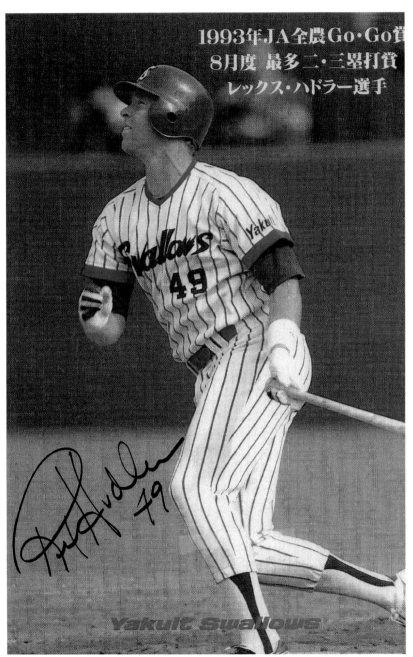

1993年JA全農Go・Go賞
8月度 最多二・三塁打賞
レックス・ハドラー選手

Playing for the Yakult Swallows in Japan.

Jennifer congratulates me after the Swallows became the
1993 Japan Series Champs.

Rex's mom, Annie
Jennifer's mom, Peggy
Jennifer, Alyssa and Me
The day we brought Alyssa home from the hospital.

A little prayer never hurts.

The best hitting coach, teacher, and friend in 21 years, the great Hall of Famer, Rod Carew. I had my best offensive years in the Majors during the three years I was with the Angels, 1994-1996. No wonder! He's the greatest!

Front row: Mark Langston, Gary DiSarcina, and Chili Davis
Back row: Bruce Hornsby and me

One afternoon in East Los Angeles filming a music video, "Walk in the Sun"
with the Great Bruce Hornsby for his album "Hot House". We're still good
friends.

Always ready to attack!

I absolutely loved turning double plays to help my pitcher out. Vizcaino tried to get me but nobody could!

Lock and load!

Another swing and miss

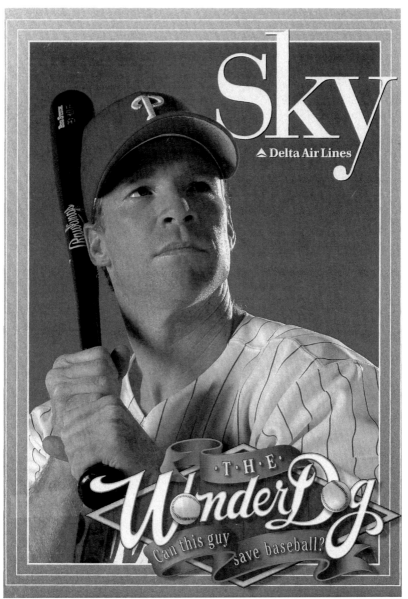

I was "sky high" with opportunities after signing with the Phillies in 1997.

I had a blast playing for the Fightin' Phils.

1997
Alyssa loves her little brother, Cade.

All my children are special, but I thank God for Cade who has brought us
valuable lessons about unconditional love.

Steve Physioc and I before an Angels game. He's been a great broadcast partner!

After the 2002 World Championship, there were opportunities galore! A visit to the Oval Office with George W. Bush. He was getting a full dose of me! My friend and fellow broadcaster, Terry Smith, and producer-engineer, Darren Chan, were probably saying, "Oh no, not another Hud story!"

In 2007 the Anaheim Ducks brought the Stanley Cup by the Angels broadcast booth.

Sweet Alyssa.

Cade headin' for home.

Will the Thrill.

David, our littlest Angel.

This is our future! Praise God! David, Will, Cade, and Alyssa.

Doin' what I love, talkin' baseball.

AND BABY MAKES 3 . . .

Dusty Baker, manager of the San Francisco Giants, picked me up as a free agent in 1994, but I did not have a guaranteed contract. They had no idea what they were getting since I'd been out of major league baseball for a year while I was playing in Japan.

The first week of spring training I was in great shape. I met up with Barry Bonds on my first day as a SF Giant. I'd battled against Barry in his Pittsburgh days and I always played the Pirates tough when I played for the Cards and the Expos so he had a lot of respect for me. I came in the locker room two days before camp opened and he rushed over to me. "Hud! Dude! We're finally on the same team." He picked me up, hugged me and then he shook me like I was a rag doll. I thought he was going to hurt me before I even put on a Giant uniform! I was in awe of his strength back then. People don't seem to understand that Barry Bonds is the best hitter of our time—with or without steroids.

I was running sprints in the early workouts and he was calling me "White Lightning" because I was so fast, and I was feeling good. I was running with turf shoes on and I developed plantar fasciitis (pain in the underside of the heel) before the Cactus League games even started. I played through it but I was in a lot of pain. I finally admitted to the trainers that I had pain in my heel, but I still had to make the team because I didn't have a guaranteed contract. I was getting cortisone shots to keep me in the lineup and time was running out. After all, my first child was due and I had to make a living.

While I was in camp with the Giants, I ran into my old buddy, Randy Johnson, my minor-league roommate when I was with the Expos. I hadn't seen him for five or six years and he started reciting everything off the back of his baseball card. "Hud, I've been Cy Young. I've won strikeout titles." Blah, blah, blah.

"Hey, Unit, that's great; I'm trying to make this ballclub. Could you give me a fastball to hit, first pitch?"

"Okay, Hud, you got it!" I was leading off against RJ and I got a first-pitch fastball about letter-high and I hit it on the screws and the first baseman grabbed it—so much for a chance to improve my spring batting average.

I could play seven positions for Dusty. He had no idea how much I'd learned in Japan because I was playing hurt and hit only about .230 for the Giants that spring. One week before the season started in '94, Wendell Kim, the Giants third base coach, tapped me on the shoulder and told me Dusty wanted to see me.

On my way over to his office I thought he was going to tell me I'd made the team, that I could help in a lot of ways and be a role player for the Giants in '94. Bob Quinn, the GM, was sitting there and Dusty was standing up behind his desk. I'm a professional at reading body language and I felt that something was wrong about his standing that way.

"Dang, Hud, I was looking forward to you making our ballclub but we're going to go with a young player by the name of John Patterson. We have to release you."

So I was out of a job again and my daughter, Alyssa, was due to be born any day. I was excited about the birth of my first child and I decided to take the high road in dealing with Dusty. "Dusty, what a pleasure it was to play for you. You're one of the best managers in the game. I also got to be team-mates with Barry Bonds, Matt Williams and Rob Thompson. The biggest thrill was that I got to meet Willie Mays, Orlando Cepeda, and Vida Blue. I grew up in the San Joaquin Valley in Fresno and always followed the Giants. Fresno is Giants country! These guys were some of my heroes!"

"Hud, you're making me feel bad about doing this." (Dusty told me later that it was Quinn's decision to cut me from the roster.)

Then Quinn said, "Rex, would you like to work for me when your career is over?"

"Wait a minute. Is this a fire and hire meeting?" I asked. "I'm going to play a bit longer, but thanks for the offer."

Typically, when you get released, you clean out your locker and you go home but I wanted to take BP and say goodbye to my teammates. I told them all, "I had a really good time playing with you but I'm going to have to find another team." They were shocked because all of the guys thought I was going to make the team. "I'm being released, but I just want to tell you how much fun I had playing with you."

Robby Thompson was amazed at how I was handling the situation. "Hud, you're acting like you got a promotion or a raise. Why are you acting like that?"

"Robby, I'm confident in my ability. I want to give my foot a little rest so it can heal and any day now I'm going to be a dad for the first time!"

I asked Murph, the famous equipment manager for the San Francisco Giants, if I could keep my jersey. "Kid, you can take everything in your locker—take it all!"

I had been wearing Will Clark's No. 22 on my back—he had just left the team the year before. I asked for Clark's number because I wanted him to know that someone who played with his same intensity was honoring his number. I called Will and told him that I had his jersey. "Oh Hud, I'm so proud that you're wearing my number!" said "Will the Thrill".

I went back to our apartment in Scottsdale and Alyssa arrived the very next day. God had this planned. The day after Alyssa was born, Bill Bavasi, the Angels first-year GM, came to our hospital room to offer me a big-league contract. He left his card with Jennifer while I was out getting lunch and told me to get back in touch. My old friend, Buck Rodgers, was now the Angels manager and he knew I could hit lefties.

AND BABY MAKES 3 . . .

When I got back from lunch Jennifer told me the news. In disbelief I said, "Honey, I know having a baby can be very traumatic. Maybe you're dreaming, seeing angels and all but..." She showed me his card and I knew it wasn't a dream.

ANGEL TALES

Arn had already negotiated a verbal agreement with the Atlanta Braves when I called to tell him about the visit from Bill Bavasi. In the Atlanta deal I would start in Richmond (AAA) to play my way back into shape which I wasn't crazy about doing. So, Arn got in touch with the Angels and we ended up sealing a deal for a great base salary and an incentive for every plate appearance I made.

(I had no way of knowing my season would end with only 170 at bats when the baseball strike hit on August 11, 1994. I went into the long, off-season with a little bit of extra cake thanks to the good deal that Arn negotiated.)

When the '94 season began, I was facing Randy Johnson and the Seattle Mariners. It was the first time I'd seen him since my attempt to make the SF Giants back in spring training. Now I was playing in the AL for real. First time up, I got a base hit. Second time up, base hit again. I had two solid singles. Third time up, I faked a bunt and RJ walked to home plate. He said, "Swing the bat, puss!" I couldn't believe he would say that to me. Now that's when he woke me up! It's on! I couldn't wait to get back into the batter's box. On the next pitch I tomahawked the ball off the right-field wall for a double and almost hit it out for a home run. Jay Buhner took it off the wall and almost threw me out at second. I was dusting myself off and Randy walked off to the back of the mound and hollered at me, "I'm keeping you in the game." I yelled, "Get back on that launching pad! We're not done with you!"

After the game, we flew back to Anaheim from Seattle and my friend, Buck Rodgers, was fired. I was bummed. Marcel Lachemann, the former Angels pitching coach, was hired by our GM, Bill Bavasi, as our new manager. I think Bavasi wanted someone he could trust; Buck Rodgers had treated him like he was a kid.

I was driving to the ballpark before the next game with the Mariners, just knowing that I was going to be in the lineup because we were facing RJ again, but my name was not on the lineup card. I went to Marcel's office and asked him, "Is it better for the team today that you're going with someone else? You weren't here last week but I went 3-4 against this guy."

"I'm going with Bo Jackson today, Hud. I know you raked RJ last time."

"No problem! I just want to know how to be a good player for you today." I had been sincere and said to myself, "Come on Hud, Bo Jackson is one of the greatest athletes ever."

That was my style. If I had something I needed to get off my chest, I'd go talk to the manager about it first thing—that way I could be a good teammate the rest of the day. You see a lot of poison in the game of baseball; if you're in a bad mood you bring other guys down. Being negative wasn't in my repertoire. I didn't like to spread poison.

When RJ came out to take some warm-up tosses in the third inning and he looked into the Angels dugout, he raised his arms up wondering why I wasn't in the lineup. I stood up and pointed to the manager and shook my head. But I had a bat in my hands from the first inning on, just in case. I wanted some of him so badly that I was making sawdust out of the bat!

Harold Reynolds, a prankster and Angels teammate, came over to me and passed me a note that he said came over from a Mariners batboy:

Hud,
Are you scared?
--Big Unit

Ah, that nearly drove me crazy! I was so worked up that I believed the note was real. In the ninth inning Marcel called my name to pinch hit against RJ. I jumped up and almost ran to the plate! First pitch, a fastball that I fouled straight back. Second pitch, another fastball that I fouled right back too. It was an 0-2 count and as he walked down to get a new ball from the ump, RJ said, "slider."

He didn't even have time to turn around and I yelled at him: "Throw me a belt-high fastball and see how far I hit it."

Randy heard what I said and so did Dan Wilson, the Mariners catcher. Randy shook Wilson off and now I had no idea what pitch was coming. I was burnt toast! Wilson had called for the fastball because he heard what I said, but RJ stuck with his nasty slider and got a called strike three. I calmly turned around, grabbed my pants and did a curtsy to him as if to say, "You puss. Throw me the fastball!"

The next day I went into Marcel Lachemann's office to apologize because I wanted to let Lach know that my exchange with RJ was personal and I didn't mean to disrespect the game. Marcel said, "I was wondering what you were doing." And I told him it was just a personal thing between RJ and me and that I was sorry.

One of the highlights of my first few seasons in Anaheim was playing with Bo Jackson at his peak of media hype. I remember after the Northridge earthquake we had construction crews in "The Big A" to rebuild the scoreboard. One of the iron workers had written on one of the beams: "Bo knows iron!" One day an iron worker was waving at Bo in front of that sign at the very top of the stadium and one of our guys yelled, "Bo, that guy wants a baseball." We told Bo to throw a ball to the guy—all the way up to the top of the stadium.

Bo walked to the warning track and—without any warm-up tosses—threw a ball all the way to the iron worker at the top of the stadium. It hit him right in the hands and the guy dropped it. Incredible! We could not believe it. He had a great arm. So he picked up another ball and threw it to the guy and this time it sailed over his head at the top of the stadium.

We didn't have an accurate perspective on how amazing this feat was until later that day. Chuck Finley, a great pitcher for the Angels for many years, was playing long toss in the outfield. He had thrown his 25 balls and was all stretched out and he said, "I'll do what Bo did—watch this!" He took a ball and threw it and it barely made it to the second deck.

That year was the end of the road for Bo's baseball career. He had an artificial hip and could barely walk, let alone run. He did steal one base that year though, and they stopped the game because he pulled the bag out of the ground to keep as a souvenir.

Bo used to drive his Harley to the park, roll through the security gate in the outfield and park his hog in front of the dugout. Then he'd just walk into the clubhouse to get ready for BP. The clubhouse kid would take the bike to the parking lot and then bring it down to him at the dugout when Bo was ready to leave right after the game!

Bo was a great teammate! I remember driving up next to him on the freeway and waving at him—what a sight – Bo with his skull cap on in a leather vest with those huge arms bulging out!

When the strike deadline arrived on August 11, I was hitting .302. It was the first year in the big leagues that I was batting over .300. I was out of the lineup that last pre-strike game and I was bumming out on the bench. In the ninth inning the bases were loaded and Billy Brewer was on the mound for the Kansas City Royals. I was told to pinch hit so I grabbed a bat and I quickly got a 2-0 count—the game was on the line. I had a chance to be a hero and keep my .300 average if I could come through. The count went to 3-0 and I stepped out of the box and said to myself, "Hud, dig yourself—you're going to hit .300!"

I dug back in against Brewer and two swinging strikes later I'm in a 3-2 count. I stepped out and this time said to myself, "Okay! What's coming here? Focus!" Brewer threw me another nasty hook and I swung and missed. I walked off the field and my average dipped to .298.

We went out on strike that night and that was the end of the season. It was a very depressing day for me and it was a very dark day for baseball. In fact, I got sick after the game because I was so depressed. I can assure you that the players never expected that Bud Selig would cancel the World Series. It was one of the most depressing days of my life – one of my biggest splinters!

In '95 we reported late to camp after the strike was finally resolved and I had earned a two-year contract. The owners had tried playing with scabs (replacement players) for six weeks and that was a failure. Marcel Lachemann and his coaches were forced to work with the scabs and it wore them out. When we showed up for a second spring camp the manager and coaches were already tired. The post-strike camp was a tough time. Marcel was a very serious, hard-ass type of manager to begin with and now he was even more of a drill sergeant. He yelled at me during stretching because I guess I wasn't being serious enough about the drills. We could sense his anger. Stretching had always been the players' bull session.

One of the spring training rituals was having the coaches go through how to run the bases. Rick Burleson, a former player that I greatly respected, was the Angels' coach that spring and was working on these drills. He kept comparing us to the scabs and was saying things like, "Those guys really worked hard on their base running." By the time we'd worked our way around the infield to practice making turns at the third-base bag, I was very disturbed by these comparisons. This was the way I made my living. I was a professional and I was offended.

The next day the players were running around the bases and Burleson made the same type of remark about the scabs working so hard. Before we took BP, I pulled him aside, and I said, "Rick, if you compare me one more time with some scab, then you and me are going to have some problems!" He apologized profusely, but I told him, "Rooster, don't ever do that again or we're 'gonna go'." There was a lot of friction between players and management after the strike of '94.

The mood was lightened by one of the best moments in baseball that took place on September 6, 1995. There was a big series at Camden Yards that first weekend in September. Cal Ripken of the Baltimore Orioles was attempting to tie and break Lou Gehrig's all time record for consecutive games played.

I was playing second base that day for the California Angels. Marcel Lachemann let me start against right-hander, Mike Mussina, which was unusual because I only faced left-handed pitchers. It was unbelievable to be a part of that historic game. Anybody who was anybody was there that night; President Clinton, Joe DiMaggio, Earl Weaver, Eddie Murray, the governor of Maryland, and a bunch of politicians and Hall of Famers. After the fifth inning, a major league game is official so we were all waiting for that to happen. When that inning was over, Cal had broken the record by playing 2,131 consecutive games!! His teammates pushed him out of the dugout to take a victory lap. To my knowledge, it was the only victory lap taken in baseball in the middle of a game. I was just standing on 2nd base in awe.

The Rawlings Company had made special baseballs stitched in orange with Cal's #8 on them for this game. The only way you could keep one of the balls was if you caught the 3rd out of an inning or a foul ball.

When Cal came to the plate there were 2 outs and 3 men on base. I was praying, "Please hit it to me." Sure enough! On the first pitch, Cal flared a ball in shallow right center and as I took off for the ball, I said to myself, "Oh my gosh, I've gotta catch it! There it is!" I ran for that ball like it was a 5 carat diamond. I caught it and shook it like I had the winning prize 'cause I got the souvenir of a lifetime. It was a huge keepsake. The Angels were in a pennant race and I saved two runs too!

I ran right by my teammates who were reaching up to give me high-fives. I wanted to secure my souvenir in my bag in the locker room!

After the game, I was "holding court" (talking) with the media by my locker. A bat boy appeared with a bat. It was from Cal! I was a bat collector and I had asked Cal for a bat a year earlier, but he never gave me one. I had told Mark Langston on our way to Baltimore that I had a feeling Cal was gonna come through with a bat on this trip. Mark said, "Hud, I know you think a lot of yourself, but what makes you think Cal's gonna be thinking of you on this big weekend?"

I said, "Hey look, he's a class act. You just wait and see." Sure enough!

When the bat boy handed me that bat, it was like Christmas morning! Cal wrote:

"Rex, you know it's been a long time since we broke in (you going ahead of me in the draft) until this date. Right now I'm feeling like when you strike out with the bases loaded; visibly shaken." Cal Ripken, September 6, 1995

I cherish the bat and ball although 2-year old Alyssa "autographed" the ball with a black sharpie before Cal had a chance to sign it!

The season went on and the Angels had a very good hitting team in '95 and played well for most of the year but as a team we tanked an 11-game lead in August. We had five games left to play and Seattle had a three-game lead.

We squared off against the Oakland A's at "The Big A" and had to face Todd Stottlemyre and Steve Ontiveros, two very good pitchers. Our backs were up against the wall so Marcel took me off the bench and gave me the regular job at second base. The Angels went on to sweep the A's to set up a one-game playoff against Seattle!

We had to face Randy Johnson in Seattle, all the hype of the playoff, and one of the loudest crowds I'd ever encountered. It was a do-or-die game pitting Randy Johnson against Mark "Langley" Langston. Langston had been traded to Montreal for RJ, and Mark came back to the Angels via free agency. I was sitting next to Langley on the way to the ballpark and I told him that no matter what happened we must act like pros and keep our heads up.

The game was a battle. Randy had a no-hitter for seven innings and was mowing people down. He was throwing 100 mph. I came up in the seventh inning and hit a fastball between Joey Cora at second base and Tino Martinez at first base and broke up his no-hitter. I yelled out to RJ as I was running to first base: "Not today, Unit. Not today!"

The crowd went nuts. RJ was shaking his head on the way back to the mound. Seattle broke open the game in the 7th inning and Langston ended up face down on the ground after a play at the plate. I thought he was hurt but he was just bummed out. I was saying to myself, "Get up Langley; don't let them see you doing that!" Right after that he was pulled from the game and he had his head in a towel in the dugout.

I was really angry with him and so when the inning was over I went over to Langley and said, "Get your f--#?/% head up; that looks like s--#?/%." I was only telling him that to remind him of what we had talked about before the game. I didn't think he would take it personally. I didn't realize it was the biggest game of his career. I wasn't thinking. I wasn't tactful. Bad splinter!

He started cussing at me! I had to regain my focus because I was about to hit again. After I came back to the dugout the next inning he followed me down to the bat rack and really let me have it. I just touched his leg; I couldn't make eye contact or we might have gone to blows. I asked him to forgive me the next inning for saying those things. "Langley, I made a mistake and I'm sorry because I don't want that to come between us and our friendship." Just like that, we were brothers again.

"Hud, no problem—it's over!"

After the game the media was coming over to my locker and questioned me about the outburst. I went over to Langston and warned him that the media was going to grill him about what happened and he asked me what I had told them.

"I was just trying to encourage you," is what I said.

"Thanks, Hud, that's a crock!"

After we had lost the one-game playoff and I was walking across the field, with my ears ringing from all the noise, I said to myself that something good would come from what happened. It was a great win for the city of Seattle, and so before I left the field I decided to get over my disappointment.

Because of that win the Mariners didn't move to Tampa and because of their post-season success that followed, (they beat the Yankees after they beat us), they got Safeco Field built. I feel partly responsible for that great stadium.

I called Jim Rome on his show the next day to give him the inside information on the game. Rome asked me, "Hud, what did you say to Mark that made him so mad?" I said I was just trying to encourage him in so many words. Well, Langley and his family were driving in the car and just happened to be listening to "The Jim Rome Show" while I was doing my interview. Mark wanted people to hear the real story. Mark's daughter, Katie, and her class at school were watching that one-game playoff on TV and she saw her daddy saying bad words to me. So he was hacked at me that the story I was telling wasn't the truth. He was embarrassed. So, after I did the radio show, Rome's producer called me to say he had someone on the other line claiming to be Mark Langston.

"Ask him what I said yesterday."

"Get your f--#?/% head up; it looks like s--#?/%!"

"That's him. Put him on the air."

Langston had never been on the Rome show before, but now he had to set the story straight. "I heard that interview you did with Hud, and he's a great guy but I just want to go on record to say that he was wrong. He was off base and I'm tired of him making me look bad. He hurt my feelings."

This was like therapy for my pain. I needed to get this out in the open. He was the one who told Rome the truth about what I said and it was perfect. We basically made up with each other on a nationally-syndicated radio broadcast.

After that interview I called Langley and said, "That was awesome! You were great! Way to set the record straight and you went into 'The Jungle' to do it—nice!"

BUILDING NEW DREAMS

In '96 the Angels struggled but it was an exciting year for me personally because Jennifer and I were expecting another child. I hit well in spring training, including a grand slam off Troy Percival during an intrasquad game. I had tremendous confidence after my success down the stretch in '95, and the new baby was coming in the fall.

Like most parents over 30, we did the necessary blood work and everything was normal except one test came back that we had a 1 in 300 chance of having a child with Down syndrome. Jennifer and I prayed about whether we should do an amnio, which puts the fetus at a slight risk and decided against it because I trusted God for what He was going to give us. Besides, if we had the amnio and determined that the baby had an abnormality, what would we do with the baby? We'd keep it, of course. So my attitude was, "Let's trust God with what He would give us".

I had a very good season in '96 though the Angels didn't make the playoffs. I was a free-agent and I had my best season, a .311 batting average with 16 home runs and 20 doubles. I put up those numbers in just over 300 at bats, and when you project them over a full year it's clear that I'd had a productive season. I was getting interest from the Dodgers,

Cleveland and the Phillies. It came down to two teams—the Phillies and the Dodgers, who were offering the best package.

Meanwhile, our second child Cade (named for my great-grandfather) was born on November 4, 1996. Jennifer's water broke in the car on our way to Saddleback Memorial Hospital. I was driving a Pontiac Bonneville—a great car, very fast -- and she was yelling that the baby was trying to come out right then and there. I was doing 120 mph and thank God it was 1:00 AM. and there was no traffic. By the time we got to the hospital she was screaming!

I parked at the ER entrance, ran in and told the woman at the front desk (who didn't quite believe me) how urgent things were getting. "My wife is having a baby!" "Yes, Sir," she said rather nonchalantly. Then she looked over my shoulder and I saw her eyes light up as she saw Jennifer wad-dling in and by this time Cade was crowning. The lady grabbed the wheelchair and they wheeled Jennifer through the dark, shadowy hallways of the hospital. Cade was coming out and I yelled, "Doc, let's go! This baby is coming out!" I was freaking out! They put her on the bed, the doctor came running in and Cade was delivered six minutes later! I cut the umbilical cord. It was an exciting moment, but I noticed that Cade didn't cry. I asked the nurse if everything was okay and she ignored me as she took him over to the hot tray or whatever they put the new babies on and a little yellow light went on in my head. However, I quickly let that go, as I saw a beautiful little boy that had my athletic booty and my red hair. I got excited! And yet -- he didn't cry.

We took Cade back to the room and like a lot of babies, he had a hard time latching on and wasn't nursing well. They brought in a lactation specialist to help Jennifer and Cade learn to feed.

Jennifer told me they were circumcising him that morning and I wanted to be there. They clipped him and -- he still didn't cry. The nurse exclaimed, "What a tough boy!"

The pediatric doctor made his rounds and looked at Cade and pronounced him a typical, healthy, baby boy. We were supposed to take him home the next day and yet he still hadn't nursed properly and -- he still had not cried. Something did not feel right to me.

At one point during the night, the on-duty nurse made an off-hand comment to Jennifer that Cade didn't have the traits of a child with Down syndrome. This was news to my wife. Where was this remark coming from? Jennifer called me up at 2:00 AM crying. She said, "Honey, there might be something wrong with Cade." She told me what the nurse had said to her and I told her I would call the doctor. She said, "No, wait until morning—it's too late." I told her okay, but after I hung up the phone, I immediately called her doctor and asked, "Doc, is there something you're not telling us about our son because one of your nurses just said something about Down syndrome to my wife?"

The doctor, Marc Winter, a fabulous doctor and friend,

was angry about the nurse making the comment. He said there was no way to tell anything from looking at Cade because his facial features were typical. To put our minds at ease, a blood test was ordered. They pricked Cade's toe and drew some blood the day we were taking him home — he still didn't cry, but we did!

We had all the nice flowers and the usual baby stuff to load in the car after you have a newborn, but we were taking him home under a cloud of concern. When we got home there was a sign made by my thoughtful Aunt Mina on the garage door that read: "Welcome Home, Cade!" I got out of the car, looked to see if anyone was watching me, and I pulled the sign down. I was very choked up. It should have been one of the happiest days of my life and it turned into an internal struggle of conflicting emotions. At that moment I understood how parents might feel when they bring home a child without knowing if there is something wrong.

We were told the blood work could take up to 15 days to determine anything but I pleaded with the doctor to call us as soon as he found out what was going on. My mom and Jennifer's mom were staying with us to help out. The phone rang two days after we got home and we were told that we had a child with Down syndrome.

"Thanks for letting us know so quickly, but is there an owner's manual? What are we supposed to do?" We were given a few phone numbers of county service agencies and that was about the extent of the help we were given.

We got off the phone and told our family the news and everyone started crying. But I stayed strong. "It's no problem. Everything is okay." My grandpa called and he was weeping like a child. I'd never seen or heard my grandpa cry before in my life. But I told him that everything would be okay. I was trying to be the strong one in the family.

After a day or so I needed some advice from somebody. I really wanted to talk to someone who knew what I was going through. I decided to call my friend Tim Burke, an ex-teammate and the closer for the Montreal Expos. He and his wife, Christine, had adopted kids with special needs. One of Tim's children became mentally disabled through a heart procedure, so I thought he could possibly give me some badly-needed encouragement. I got him on the first call and said, "Burkie, hey, it's Hud. Jennifer and I just found out that our new child has Down syndrome. Do you have any advice?"

"Yeah, Hud, you need to grieve with Jennifer." He confided that he and his wife, Christine, had problems in their relationship because Tim had been unable to grieve. I told him thanks and hung up the phone and I cried with Jennifer for two days. I finally let my emotions come on out. We had to grieve the loss of the dreams we had for a typical child. We had to build new dreams for our son Cade. At the time, I felt a deep splinter.

The next day I had to go back to the gym because I'd been off for a week after the birth of my son. I walked into the gym and there were Mark Langston, Chuck Finley, J.T. Snow and Jim Abbott asking me, "Hud, tell us about your new baby!" It was one of the hardest things I ever had to do—to tell them that Cade had Down syndrome, and I wept in front of my guys. They hugged me and offered me their love and support.

Later that day I was doing cardio in the training room, and Jim Abbott was next to me on his treadmill and we were walking side by side. Jim Abbott, if you recall, had pitched a no-hitter for the Yankees, even though he only had one hand. He told me, "Hud, miracles can happen. You stay with Cade; you and Jennifer are going to be great parents for him. Help him reach his full potential."

I was blindsided with a left hook. This inspiration was coming from the perfect source. What impressed me about Jim was his humility. He didn't say, "Look what I did with my disability." He simply said, "Miracles can happen!"

I had never had a seven-day period of depression like this one in my life. God was telling me that this had been a mourning time and the time to mourn was at an end. God said to me, "Hud, I'm going to start bringing you out of the dark time now. I'm going to start bringing some special people around you to bring you up. I'm going to start pumping you up." First, was the love I got from the my teammates. Then, Jim Abbott encouraged me with his message: "Miracles can happen."

Jim didn't tell me how he had achieved miracles. He

didn't praise his own achievements, though he could have because he did achieve miracles of his own. But his simple and pure statement changed my whole perspective.

Twenty minutes after I left Abbott I was back praising God and God told me, "Hud, now that you're back to being Hud again I'm going to tell you why I brought Cade into your life. I didn't give you this son to bring your life down; I gave you this child to enhance your life! I've got big things planned for you and him. You go home and pump your wife up right now."

I went home to Jennifer, who was so depressed that she hadn't left her room for a week. I took my Bible out and read to her from the Scripture, "God has plans for our lives." Cade is our gift. What do you do when you're given a gift? You hold out your hands and say, "Thank you." God wants us to accept the gift that He gave us. Let's be thankful. We will raise this child up to his full potential. And along the way maybe we'll be able to encourage other people."

That's when we did a complete about-face and our attitude about Cade began to change. We got through our time of grieving by being with the right people, at the right place, at the right time. Only God could do that and He knew the plans He had for us.

Jennifer and I became involved with a local support group for families and children with Down syndrome. We were also meeting families of children with different disabilities where Cade received many of his services. These were services that helped him develop fine and gross motor skills, speaking and eating and social skills too. We were encouraged by these families to use the platform that I had been given to raise awareness of the positive qualities and contributions that children and adults with Down syndrome give in life. That was the beginning of our journey to form our organization, Team Up For Down Syndrome. We were simply one family wanting to help another family. We wanted then, as we do now, for people to celebrate the lives of their children, no matter what their abilities may be.

PHILLY CHEESE STEAKS

It was close to Thanksgiving when the phone rang. It was Arn Tellem letting me know that some teams wanted to give me $1 million per year for two years. Wow! I made that kind of money in Japan but I'd never made that kind of money before in my major league career in the U.S. and I was 36 years old. It boiled down to the Dodgers and the Phillies, because Cleveland dropped out of the running. I said, "Arn, let me call them!" Arn trusted me to say the right things. I called Terry Francona, the newly-hired manager of the Phillies, and asked him a question, "Are the Atlanta Braves in your division?"

"Yeah."

"Dude, there's no way you're going to finish in first place and I don't want to finish my career on a last-place team."

"Hud," he said, "I need you. I need your clubhouse presence and leadership with all the young guys (Scott Rolen and Bobby Abreu)."

"You're going to have to overpay me to play for the Phillies."

"Hud, I'll call Lee Thomas (the Phillies General Manager) and I'll get back to you."

They offered me $2.8 million for two years and I discussed it with Jennifer. It was a long way to move and a very tough place to play. She told me to call the Dodgers. Fred Claire, the Dodgers GM, said he'd call me back with an answer. I grabbed Jennifer's hand and asked the Lord to put us where He wanted us.

Right after our prayer was over, Fred called back to tell me that they couldn't match the Phillies offer. I told Jennifer that $800,000 was the difference between the two offers. She said, "We'll never see that kind of money again so we've got to go!"

I called Fred Claire back and declined his offer, "Mr. Claire, thank you so much for your interest in me. It's an honor to be wanted by a wonderful organization like the Dodgers. See ya' opening day!"

"All things work for the good of those who love God and are called according to His purpose." Rom. 8:28

I signed my contract with the Phillies, and needless to say I was very excited. Even though I was 36 years old, I was in tremendous shape. I was running as fast as I did back when I was 28 and stealing bases for the Expos with Otis Nixon.

I was working out in the gym to get ready for spring training and I was sprinting on a high-speed treadmill as part of a test in which you run 20 mph for five seconds and then you jump off. The goal of the test is to determine maximum speed. I nailed 21 mph and my peers on the Angels were amazed. "C'mon, Hud, you can do 22!" I was tired. That was enough for me. But I made the mistake of going for 22, and I had no business doing that. My trainer should have been held responsible for making that mistake; of letting me fall for that peer pressure!

I jumped on and ran about 2 seconds and pop! I popped my hamstring on that final rep at 22 mph and I quickly grabbed my gym bag and went to my car. I knew I had hurt myself. My hamstring was craving ice! I went home, iced the hamstring and hoped it would heal properly in time for spring training. I had never pulled a muscle in my entire career.

The Phillies marketing department called up me a few days later to get me to go on the Winter Caravan to promote the team. While I was in Philadelphia I showed my hamstring to "Coop," the Phillies trainer. I said, "Could I show you something?" The back of my leg was black and blue from my butt cheek all the way to my ankle.

Coop's nickname was "Mumbles." He had a big handlebar mustache and you couldn't see his lips move and it was hard to hear what he was saying. He mumbled something, put me on the Cybex machine and gave me a rehab program for January and February to get my hamstring ready for playing baseball in Clearwater, Florida.

I worked hard on the rehab and was feeling pretty good when I arrived at spring training. But during the first day of BP I took a swing and my leg buckled. I was in physical therapy the entire month of March to prepare for the season. With one week left in spring training, I was finally able to play. In the meantime, Terry Francona treated me like I was Babe Ruth. What a respectful manager! I have a special place in my heart for my Phillies skipper and the entire Phillies organization.

We opened the season on the West Coast at Dodger Stadium. We were stretching next to the batting cage and Joe Amalfitano, a Dodgers coach, was looking at me and saying, "I can't believe you chose Philly over us!" The Phillies didn't play too well and I was 0-12 on the trip to make things worse.

I was in the lineup on opening night in Philadelphia, the big free-agent signing of the off-season, and I was batting .000 after 12 at bats. I got a sawed-off base hit over the head of the shortstop. Sterling Hitchcock, a southpaw on the Padres, tried to jam me on the inside part of the plate and I hit a flare. I turned those jam-shots on turf into doubles by sprinting out of the box. When I hit that ball and I took off like a rabbit, I blew out my other hamstring. I grabbed my hamstring when I got to second base and Terry Francona, the Phillies manager, called me off the field. That was the most embarrassing, humbling time of my entire career. I limped off the field in front of 65,000 booing Phillies fans. Embarrassing splinter!

During spring training I had done a long interview with Jim Salisbury, an excellent writer for *The Philadelphia Inquirer*, about Cade and Down syndrome. The newspaper sent a photographer over to my house to snap photos of the family, and on opening day there was a big story with photos about me on Page One with a cover image of me holding Cade and nuzzling him in my arms

The article on Cade was a beautiful thing. I started getting bags of fan mail. People were sending me photos of their kids and words of encouragement, "Hey, you've got nothing to be worried about. My kid with Down syndrome graduated from high school, he's driving a car, and he's even going to college."

These letters of encouragement were pumping me up— and this was in Philly, a town that's known for the toughness of its fans, not their compassion. The Phillies had a unique bunch of characters back in the '90s: Darren "Dutch" Daulton, Curt Schilling, Mickey Morandini and Lenny Dykstra. I was sobbing in the clubhouse while I was reading some of these beautiful letters and Daulton was looking over at me while reading a newspaper. The guys on that team were all tough, hardcore ballplayers. But they embraced me and my family just like the fans had. I said, "Dutchie, I'm sorry. I don't mean to bring your clubhouse down." He said, "Hud, what you got going is real. Don't worry about it."

The article helped to make me a fan favorite during my time in Philadelphia, despite my injury problems. When I wasn't playing, I'd go down on the field and sign autographs. The fans really warmed my heart. God took us to Philadelphia for a reason. He wanted us to go to a place known for its hostility, and be lifted and loved and encouraged and in turn be able to encourage other people. Sometimes Phillies fans get a bad rap!

In 1998 I was healthy again, but things had changed in one year with the direction the Phillies were headed. They had a bunch of young kids and I could see they were moving me out. I had only 20 at bats in the first two months of the season. Morandini played second base and Kevin Stocker was at short—I was a utility player once again and hardly used at all.

I had just qualified as a 10-year major league veteran. I called the Major League Baseball Players Association to find out the exact date of my 10-year anniversary and it was on Mother's Day in '98. Praise God! That was perfect timing. My mom was such a positive force in my life. She helped me to accept my role as a utility player throughout my career. She instilled nothing but uplifting words and encouragement in me!

Mother's Day came and went and the very next day I went into Terry Francona's office and I told him, "Tito, I want you to know that I'm a fulfilled ballplayer today. Thank you."

"Hud," he asked, "What do you mean?"

"I got my 10 years in the majors in yesterday—that was my goal. After spending 10 years in the minors I told myself I'd get 10 years in the majors. And I achieved my goal yesterday. You can trade me. You can release me. Or you can send me down to the minor leagues. I'm just telling you I'm fulfilled and I'll do whatever works best for the Phillies. If you can trade me for a case of balls, do it! Oh, by the way, Tito; when you give my jersey (#14) to some young punk, tell him he could never take it from me—I'm giving it to him!"

God had a plan; it wasn't my plan, but I was letting Him drive the car once again.

The Phillies put my 10-year achievement on the scoreboard: "Congratulations, Rex Hudler! Your teammates congratulate you on your 10 years in the big leagues." That was so awesome!

One week later, we were playing in Boston and Rico Brogna was playing first base for us. He got hurt early in the game and Tito told me to take his place. It turned out to be a 2-1 win for the Phillies and Mark Portugal pitched a great game. We flew back to Philadelphia after the game and I got a call to come to the ballpark the next day. "We've made a decision on you." When I put down the phone I looked at Jennifer and asked, "What's the perfect scenario for you – a trade, a send down, or a release?" She said, "A release, so you could come home and be with the family."

I walked into Francona's office and Ed Wade, the GM, was there. I was trying to get a feel for what was going on but I could not read them. I knew they couldn't be happy since the team was not playing well and I was riding the bench and not hitting. I knew I wasn't getting a promotion or anything good.

Francona said they were releasing me, that they were

going to let me go home!

"I'm sorry. It was my fault that I messed up my hamstring. If I hadn't been hurt I would have been the player that you paid for."

Francona told me to forget about it. "Hud, you did what we paid you for. We brought you over here to babysit our young players (Scott Rolen, Mike Lieberthal, Bobby Abreu, and Desi Relaford). We had 13 rookies on the team. Hud, you did a great job working with the kids. You've been a real pro. You lifted the kids up to play the game the right way."

The biggest compliment is that Scott Rolen, Bobby Abreu and the guys still playing 10 years later all come up to me now and treat me like a father figure or a big brother. It's important that veteran players pass the game on to the young guys!

BUFFALO WINGS

I went to the gym to work out that afternoon of my release and I was already getting calls from the Cleveland Indians and the St. Louis Cardinals. I was happy that I was still a player other teams wanted on their roster.

Jennifer asked me, "Do you have baseball out of your system."

"What do you mean?"

"Do you have playing baseball out of your system? I've got to live with you the rest of your life so get playing out of your system!"

"You know what—not really. Hearing from these other teams is getting me excited. My speed is good. I'm 100% healthy. I'm still a good player."

We decided to go with Cleveland because I could hit well against Andy Pettitte, David Wells and the other top south-paw hurlers in the AL. The Indians were going to have face Pettitte and Wells in the playoffs and that made me an asset. They took a chance for nothing which began one of my final baseball splinters.

The Indians sent me to Buffalo (AAA) in early June. My timing was off from not playing for two months in Philadelphia, and I was hitting about .130 after 14 days. I was in my 15th day in Buffalo and some fan yelled out, "Hudler, you're a bum. Your hustle is great, but show us some numbers!" I shook my head up and down. I had to agree. I always agreed with cat calls from the fans. Those guys paid my salary. Whenever someone called me a bum, I would say, "I know, but he keeps on playing me!"

Right then and there my heart said to retire from baseball. God gave me the conviction that I was ready to leave. I went into the dugout and asked Bud Black, the pitching coach at Buffalo and now the Padres manager, what it was like when he retired at 38. "My arm felt great but I couldn't get anybody out," he told me. I couldn't hit anything and hearing what Buddy had to say helped me make my decision.

After the game I went into talk to the manager, Jeff Datz, now the Cleveland Indians bench coach. I said, "I'm sorry for taking a roster spot that should belong to a young player but it's time for me to go home. I feel it in my heart that the timing is right."

"Hud, we didn't care what you hit here in Buffalo. You were going to be called up to Cleveland because you are a fun guy to have in the clubhouse."

"I got my 10 years in the big leagues and that was my goal. I have to listen to my heart and call it a career. But can you let me play second base tomorrow? I love day games and want to finish my career after playing my favorite position (second base), and I'd like to address your team before the game."

Jeff Datz said, "Hud, you got it."

Then I told Jennifer on the phone that night I was coming home.

"Are you sure? Don't come home if you're not ready. I know you're scuffling right now but please be sure this is what you want," said my soul mate. Jennifer was so smart to make sure I wasn't going to change my mind and be sorry a year or two later. She needed to know I had the conviction from God to move on with my life. But my plan was to play one more game and fly home.

That night I had dreams that I'd end my career like Ted Williams and hit a home run in the last at bat of my final game. This was my final game after 21 years of pro ball and for me—and only me—it was a big deal. I was in my own little world. I was going to leave the game I loved on my own terms. It was a blessing.

I was on the phone doing the Jim Rome show to tell him and all the Jungle I was retiring from baseball after the game. I called him from the clubhouse to talk about the end of my career, how it felt in my heart to walk away from baseball, and I was thanking Jim and thanking God.

I addressed the team before my final game, "Hey, fellas, I just want to tell you I'm leaving today. I'm retiring from baseball after 21 years. Let me tell you how much joy I've had in playing baseball. I've played since I was 17 and I'm going to share some of the things that will keep you in the big leagues and some of things that will keep you out. You

SPLINTERS

have to be focused and have a passion for the game. You have
to come to the yard every day wanting to play the game and
try to better yourself and the people around you. Be a fountain, not a drain. I want to go out a winner so let's play some
ball! Let's attack and play this game!" I was almost like John
Belushi in his famed Animal House speech.

The National Anthem was hard to get through, as I was
weeping like a small child. I was standing next to the shortstop, Enrique Wilson, praising God and praying for
Enrique. He was looking at me boo-hooing, and I guarantee
he'll never experience an anthem like that one again!

I struck out in my first at bat. I was walking off the field
and thinking—perfect time to leave, Hud. You suck! I got a
base hit to left in my next at bat. Tony Tarasco, a pretty good
defensive outfielder, was in left field that day. I took my turn
around first base—did they think I'd actually stop at first in
my last game ever? No way! I sped into second and did a
hook-slide under the tag and was safe but the umpire called
me out. I got a big, beautiful strawberry from that play. I got
my battle scar, my souvenir. I was taking high-fives from my
teammates after getting thrown out. I was safe, but I didn't
care. I had never gotten high-fives for making an out before.
My team loved it!

Now, it was my third at bat and something out-of-the-
way happened. In my entire 21-year professional baseball
career, I'd never been hit by a pitch in the head. I'd had 95-
mph fastballs whiz by my head and I could always get out of

130

the way. On my last day in pro ball, I dug in and got a fast-ball from Scott Ruffcorn, my ex-teammate with the Phillies, and I saw this ball coming right at my dome! I turned my head and the ball hit me right in the neck! I got "necked"!

I put my hands on my knees and looked down at home plate and I heard God's voice louder than I'd ever heard it before, "I TOLD YOU TO LEAVE LAST NIGHT!" That was the message He sent me. "I put it on your heart to get out and you took it upon yourself to play another game. I've got something else planned for you. You got to go!"

I lifted my head up and sprinted down to the first base bag. The 3,000 fans that day were trippin' and my team-mates were going, "Look at Hud—he's a freak. He just got hit in the head and he's sprinting down the line." It was my last game. I had pride in the game and I couldn't cheat it.

The inning was over and I went out to second base to take groundballs for warm-ups and I felt an enormous knot swelling up behind my ear. It was a knot the size of a golf ball and I knew it could be something serious so I ran off the field. I got to the dugout and Jeff Manto yelled at me, "Hud, you're not coming out of the game, are you?" It was peer pressure. I couldn't end my career that way so I grabbed a towel, wiped my face and sprinted back to second base. As far as my teammates knew I was just coming into the dugout to get a towel, but I was scared!

I went back out on the field for another inning and let a tailor-made double-play ball go right through my legs for an error. In our next time at bat, leading 18-2, the manager looked at me and said, "Hud, you're on deck." I told him to stick a fork in me—I'm done! I did not want to go up to the plate again after what God told me the last time. So that's how I decided to end my 21-year career—by getting hit in the neck! Painful splinter!

The game ended and I was surrounded by 25 reporters. I was shocked. Most players finish their careers and no one even cares and here I am holding a press conference after a minor-league game! I shared the joy of playing baseball with them and told a few stories. I went into the clubhouse and my teammates had little Dixie cups filled with champagne waiting for me.

On the flight back home, I thought about ending my career by getting hit on the neck and making an error. It was the perfect ending for me. I had so many battles and spent so many years struggling in the low minors. It was God's way of saying, "I have something else prepared for you, Hud, but now you got to go!" Final baseball splinter!

MR. NATURAL

Two days after my final baseball game, I got a call from Tim Mead of the California Angels asking me if I was interested in being a broadcaster.

"What? Are you serious?"

"We are a little nervous about your personality, but we think that with time and hard work you could develop into a good broadcaster."

"What are we talking about?"

"We're offering you a one-year contract with an option."

"But we just moved from Orange County to Philadelphia. We bought a home here and I can't ask Jennifer to move again for only a one-year commitment."

Tim told me he'd see what he could do to improve the deal. He called me back the next day with an offer of three years plus an option for a fourth year. I went to Jennifer and told her what was on the table.

Jennifer was pumped! "We're gone. We're going home to Orange County!"

We really enjoyed living in Philly. God had a plan and sent us so I could play for Terry Francona, a great guy, and to get pumped up by the people of Philadelphia. But quite honestly, I enjoyed all of the towns where I played major league baseball: New York, Baltimore, Montreal, St. Louis, Anaheim, and Philadelphia. Jennifer and I always made a commitment to work in each community through local charity organizations and our church.

We missed Philadelphia for many reasons, not the least of which was that we made great friends while we lived there. I kind of expected to stay in Philadelphia and work in TV and radio since my agent, Arn Tellem, had connections and I could have gotten a job with the Phillies.

But as it turned out, the timing of the move was perfect. When the Angels hired me, I went right to the big leagues of broadcasting without having to do 10 years in the minors! I was starting my next career in "The Show" even though I had no formal training.

When I was hired, the Angels had former big-league manager, Sparky Anderson, and Jerry Reuss doing the games. Since Sparky wouldn't travel with the team, they hired me to do all the road games and to work with veteran play-by-play announcer, Steve Physioc. Phys is a great guy and easy to work with.

Before signing the deal they had me do a simulated broadcast with Phys in the Fox TV Studios. They picked out a random Angels game and Phys and I did the broadcast as if it was live in the booth. The game was an Angels-Twins matchup and Allen Watson was pitching. He threw over to hold the runner at first five times and I said to Phys that if Watson wasn't careful he could lose his focus on the hitter and that could lead to serious damage. On the next pitch the hitter smacked a home run and I'd hit a home run in my audition! We did another three innings and Physioc and I clicked right away as if we'd been working together for years. That was all the Angels needed to see and the deal was signed. My second career was launched.

I'm a believer in making predictions in broadcasting if I feel something will happen in a given situation. When you make predictions and it comes true, people tend to remember. When you make a prediction and it doesn't happen, people tend to forget. I predicted Mike Napoli's first major-league home run one pitch before he hit it. It was against Justin Verlander of the Tigers and I could just feel it, so I went out on a limb and said he'd go deep.

I may have been a natural in the booth, but the first year was tough. The Angels lost 92 games in 1999 and there was a lot of turmoil surrounding the team. Terry Collins, the Angels manager who was fired during that season, didn't show me much respect. Collins knew me from our National League days when he'd been a coach for Jim Leyland with the Pirates and I was playing for Montreal and St. Louis. He was trying to be funny I think, but he was always very cutting and disrespectful to me. I showed up to broadcast a series in Boston and he yelled over at me in front of the entire team, "Oh, front runner—you only come around when we play the big teams." I took it with no problem, but a lot of guys on the team had more respect for me.

I never let the negative stuff get to me. I laughed it off. I was like a rookie player taking abuse, but I would not let it bother me. The truth was that Terry Collins didn't have great communication skills as a manager or as a person.

Rod Carew, the hitting coach under Collins that season, was a good friend of mine. We were shopping on an off day on the road and he let me know that some of the coaches and players didn't like the way Collins was treating me as a broadcaster. "This guy isn't giving you any respect, Hud, and you worked your butt off as a player for 10 years. You've earned more respect than he's been giving you."

I told Rod that it's not about me; it's about how he treats the players and the fans and deals with the community. I could handle what was thrown at me without complaining.

Collins was fired and GM, Bill Bavasi, resigned that year. The Angels were an organization in transition. During the dark times of '99 my positive personality helped a lot to improve the situation. We were getting letters from our viewers who were used to the laid back style of Sparky Anderson. "I can't sleep after I'm done watching Angels games because this Hudler guy has me wound up too tight!"

Mike Scioscia was hired as the Angels manager in 2000 and we hit it off from day one. The team made steady improvements under Scioscia and I was evolving into an analyst rather than a guy who leaned on his personality to guide the broadcast.

Some of my broadcast coaches were telling me that I had

a good personality, but that my energy and enthusiasm could also work against me. I had to learn how to contain my energy and not let it bubble over all the time. I wanted to be true to myself but I still had to learn to become an analyst.

The Angels were so good in 2002 that it made it easy to analyze the games. They were stealing bases, bunting, and playing small ball. All of a sudden they went from a second-division team to a world champions! Being in Anaheim as a broadcaster when the Angels won their first World Series in franchise history was really something special – the most fun ever!

During post-season play, I was coming to the game with my family and sitting in the stands with the fans and just talking baseball with people. I was also doing pre- and post-game interviews for local TV, but this was my chance to walk through the stands and I was getting mobbed by people.

Angels fans were in a frenzied state of mind because the team had finally made it to the World Series. I was being asked for autographs and getting mobbed by fans while walking into "The Big A" with my family. When I arrived at my seats I told Jennifer, "Honey, that crowd was very scary!"

The next day on the way to the ballpark I had a talk with myself, "Hud, you never won the World Series as a player so feel fortunate that the team you're broadcasting for now is winning games in post-season. Go with this experience and have some fun. Love those fans who are asking for your auto-graph. Don't be intimidated. You've never shied away from crowds of people before. Soak it up!"

I got out of the car and had the Sharpie in my hand. I was hugging people, signing autographs, giving fans high-fives and working them up into a frenzy. I arrived at my seats and the fans around me wanted a running commentary on the game. This was really the first time I could enjoy just being a fan, since I'd been playing baseball or broadcasting my whole life and never had a chance to sit in the stands and enjoy watching the action.

All year long I'd been calling Angels shortstop David Eckstein "The X-Factor" because he factored in on every key rally that pushed the team over the top. Now I was in the stands and Eckstein came up to the plate and the fans crossed their loud "Thundersticks" to signify that he was "The X-Factor." My wife nudged me and said, "See what you started?"

It dawned on me that I had a voice, people connected with that voice, and that I had a chance to use that voice to shape how people enjoyed and appreciated Angels baseball. I almost wept with joy to watch my "X-Factor" concept take root with the fans. I realized how important my broadcasting job is because I have a chance to entertain, educate and instruct about the game that's been a huge part of my life.

After the Angels came back to win the World Series against the San Francisco Giants, managed by my old friend Dusty Baker, I was down on the field with the crew to do post-game interviews. The team did a victory lap and a lot of the guys came over to hug me and gave me a bottle of champagne. I jumped up on the top of the dugout and started spraying fans with champagne! Getting the opportunity to connect with the players and the fans was a wonderful experience, one I'll never forget!

BASEBALL CHAPEL

I always attended Baseball Chapel on Sunday mornings during the season. I started going to Chapel early in my minor league days while I was with the Expos. My good friend Tim Burke, a terrific relief pitcher and a believer, organized the prayer meetings. Regulars included Andy McGaffigan, Tom Foley and Tim Wallach.

Some of the other players who didn't attend Chapel would put smut books in our lockers—anything to push our buttons. But with Chapel, I wasn't afraid of taking any abuse. It was a ritual that brought players together as a family in Christ. As with anything though, it wasn't going to work for everyone. Lee Smith once blamed Baseball Chapel for his allowing a game-winning home run later that day. Baseball players are very superstitious.

There was a guy named Otis who was the visiting clubhouse attendant for the Cubs. He'd always write on the blackboard when any team came to Chicago: "My favorite team is in town." On Chapel days he'd call out, "All you heathens who were partying on Rush Street all night have a chance to redeem yourself—Chapel in 10 minutes!" That was funny because it had a lot of truth in it. Ballplayers often thought of Baseball Chapel as a way to cleanse their souls of all their sins from the night before.

Chapel was often misunderstood by some players who didn't know Christ. They didn't understand that it was an opportunity to hear the word of God and to have some fellowship during the often-stressful baseball season.

The late Pat Kelly was very active in the Baseball Chapel program while I was with the Orioles. Pat used to give Earl Weaver a hard time and tried to get him to go, but Weaver would just growl at him.

Tim Burke was a very important person in my life. It was Tim who encouraged me to grieve with my wife when Jennifer and I found out our son Cade had Down syndrome and that was a crucial step in coping with the challenges we faced as a family.

After retiring from baseball, Tim became the Chaplain for the Colorado Avalanche. He was so good at it that he was asked to organize Chapel services for all the teams. Tim now runs the Chapel program for the NHL.

Now he's reaching a sport that's a lot darker than baseball. With hockey, it's not the macho thing to show you're a Christian. It was a ministry waiting to happen. You have more power and more strength with Christ in your heart and on your side. A lot of athletes don't understand that, but Tim is instrumental in spreading the Gospel.

Besides Baseball Chapel, PAO (Professional Athletes Outreach) is another organization that's very significant to Christian ballplayers. PAO sponsors off-season conferences with guest speakers speaking from a Biblical perspective about finance, marriage, raising kids and other major issues that confront couples. Jennifer would attend the conferences with me and she would sing at some of the social events. Jennifer has recorded several Christian CDs and her music ministry is another way she serves the Lord. At the PAO conferences, Jennifer was a leader for all the women and she was a leader among the wives in the Baseball Chapel program.

These Christian groups were a tremendous amount of fun for me and my family. I can't say enough good things about the importance of PAO and Baseball Chapel in my life as a professional athlete.

Tales from "The Jungle" with Jim Rome

In 1994 after I came back from Japan, I had been cut from the San Francisco Giants at the end of spring training and a week later—after the Angels picked me up—I was raking the ball. I'd finally figured how to hit a curveball in Japan and I was killing the ball. At the end of April, I was still hitting over .400. We were in Toronto, and Paul Molitor got on second base and said to me, "Hud, are you kidding? How can you still be hitting .400 this late in the season?" I gave him a little "Flex" pose like I was a strongman.

While I was in Toronto, I got a call in my hotel from the producer of "The Jim Rome Show", Travis Rodgers. He wanted to know if I'd come on about 4:00 PM. I'd be at the ballpark by then and I told him I'd be happy to go on the show even though I didn't know who Rome was or anything about the show. Rome was just starting out then. His career soon broke out and is now a nationally syndicated show.

I got to the ballpark and my name was on the lineup card. I was excited because I wasn't expecting to play. I went into my pre-game mode and started focusing and in the meantime I forgot all about the Rome show. I blew it off

143

because I was focused on my game. I totally brain cramped.

After batting practice, I was jogging across the field and there was a lone ball about 30 yards in front of me. I looked to my left and Marcel Lachemann, my manager, who was carrying his fungo bat, was walking over to pick up that ball. All of a sudden his eyes met mine and we raced for the ball. Our competitive natures took over and we were both running full speed to the ball. I reached down with my glove to try to pick it up before he could get it and he used his fungo bat to knock the ball out of my way. The fungo bat slipped out of his hands, clipped me in the legs and I fell on my shoulder and popped my clavicle out its socket — and then it popped back in. My whole right shoulder went numb.

He apologized, and I told him it wasn't a problem. I then walked over to our shortstop, Spike Owen, and told him, "The manager just put me on the disabled list." I went into the trainer's room and told our trainer, "Hey boss, do you have an ice pack? The manager just put me on the DL." I missed infield practice—and I never missed infield practice because that was my game. Lachemann came into the clubhouse and stuck his head in the training room and saw me with an ice pack on my shoulder with a big smile on my face.

"Are you okay, Hud?"

"Nothing a few weeks on the DL won't cure, boss."

He scowled and took off—he was pissed because I had been hitting .400 and acting as his catalyst. I was the hottest hitter on the team. We flew back to Los Angeles and a club-house kid by the name of Keith Tarter, who is still with the Angels, was telling me that Jim Rome was all over me on the radio. He was saying that I got hurt because of "The Jungle Karma." The Jungle Karma brought me down because I blew off an interview.

I was dumbfounded! "Really? Who is this guy? Get him on the phone."

I called the Jim Rome show and Jim said, "And joining us now is Rex Hudler, the guy who blew us off. Hey, welcome to 'The Jungle,' and I'm sorry you got hurt but I believe it's Jungle Karma that brought you down because you blew me off the other day."

"Jim, if I would have known that bad jungle karma would have taken me out of the lineup—because I was hotter than a firecracker before I got hurt—I would have never missed your show. You must be the man if your show has so much power."

I showed love to Jim Rome. I told him how great he was and how sorry I was about missing his show. He wasn't sure about me—like a lot of people. He wasn't sure where I was coming from. I was just being myself with him on the radio and later he called me back after the segment was over and gave me his hotline phone number so I could call in when-ever I wanted.

"Are you serious? I don't think you know what you're doing."

He gave me the liberty to call his show whenever I wanted and sure enough whenever something would happen, I would call in. He loved players who had the guts to give an honest take on what was going on during a game. I'd call in and give him little tidbits of what was going on.

Here are a few highlights from my calls to the Jim Rome show:

The June Bug Story

I was playing for the Cardinals and we were getting killed 8-0 by the Mets. It was early in the game, about the third or fourth inning, and I was sitting on the top step of the dugout at Busch Stadium on a beautiful June day. All of a sudden I got hit in the head with something. I thought that a fan had thrown a peanut at me from the stands. I took my hat off and on my hat was a big bug. I mean a BIG, colorful bug. It was one of the most beautiful bugs I'd ever seen, with all the colors of the rainbow—green, red, blue and yellow. I was showing this bug to my teammates like a kid at show-and-tell in school. The bug wasn't flying away.

Tom Pagnozzi challenged me, "Hud, eat it!" I was thinking there's no way I'm going to eat this thing and then the businessman side of me started thinking, "I got a chance to make some money" so I said, "Fellas, how much money will you pay me if I eat this bug?"

Joe Magrane offered me $10. "Only ten bucks? Shake yourself. You're a big leaguer, man. I'm not eating a bug for

$10. Let's go, where's the glue?"

Next thing you know Bryn Smith offered me $100 and Frank DePino offered another $100 and all this time Whitey Herzog was watching me do my thing. I got eight guys to give me $100 and the bug still hadn't flown off my cap. They told me they had one stipulation, that I don't get the money unless I chew up the bug. And I shot back, "I don't eat anything until the cash is right in my hand." So in the middle of this game against the Mets, the guys went back in the clubhouse to dig the cash out of their valuable boxes. They slapped C-notes in my hand and I had $800 in cash. I picked that bug up off of my hat with my two fingers and put him in my mouth and chewed him like a sunflower seed—no problem! I started chewing on him and was waiting for a bitter taste but the bug tasted like bacon! Not only did I make $800 bucks for eating a bug, but it even tasted good—it was the easiest money I ever made.

I got up off the bench and showed the guys what was left of the bug, and I later found out it was a June Bug. I wish I had video of their reaction I got because here was a bunch of grown men—actually boys, looking at a chewed-up bug on my tongue. They lost it!

We came from behind and ended up beating the Mets. After the game the guys were saying, "Way to munch the rally bug, man!" And as the players were leaving they told my wife Jennifer not to kiss me. When I came out she asked me, "What have you done now, Hud?"

"All I did was eat a bug!"

"You ate a bug?

I pulled out eight $100 bills, told her that I'd made that money by eating the bug, and her eyes got big and we slapped-five, got in the car and drove home.

Eating Earthworms in Japan

I told Jack Howell about the June Bug Story while were hanging out in Japan. One morning about a week later we were out running in the rain and Jack saw an earthworm on the artificial turf field —it was at least six inches long. I have no idea how it ended up on the turf because we were nowhere near any dirt. Jack picked up the worm and yelled, "Hey, fellas, Leka-sue will eat this worm. How much money will you give him to eat this worm?"

I was not mentally prepared to eat a worm. What's Jack doing? We were on a break from running and in broken English Jack asked the guys for money. He told me, "Hud, they are going to give you 4,000 yen (about $900)." I walked around to Jack, put the earthworm in my mouth and chewed it up. Overall, the worm didn't taste bad—it was like protein in its purest form! Then I started doing push-ups and clapping between reps and looking at my guys. The Japanese guys were cracking up just like my friends on the St. Louis Cardinals. My morale-boosting antics worked in any language or country. And once again I made good money. They had a rookie collect the money and the cash came to $1000.

The workouts were over and we went into the clubhouse (the media is not allowed in the clubhouse in Japan). As I walked out on the street there were 150 photographers with smiles on their faces waiting to take my picture saying, "Oshi! Oshi!" (which means good) I realized that they must have heard the worm-eating story and so I took a toothpick out of my coat pocket and started picking my teeth and I rubbed my belly. The next day I made the front page of all seven newspapers in Japan, and the headlines read: "Crazy American Eats Worm." My new nickname was "The Worm Man." All these years later, the Japanese fans only remember me for eating worms, not the Japanese championship I helped Yakut win! But at least they remember me for something!

NASCAR

Jim Rome has not always been a NASCAR fan and I was one of the people who changed his mind about it. I went out and took a courtesy ride in Fontana on the super track to race a car at 170 mph with an instructor. It was such a thrilling experience that I had to call Rome on the hotline, "Romy, you'll never believe this! I got a ride in one of those NASCARs. It was off the charts! You'll become a fan if you go out and drive one of those cars!"

I told him how the instructor kept pulling my leg off the throttle because I was going too fast. And Jim started tossing out the names of all the drivers on the circuit and doing his best impersonation of me talking about Petty and Earnhardt and all the other top drivers. And the next thing you know, he warmed up to NASCAR. Now he treats it like a sport.

Cade Hudler

Cade was born on November 4, 1996, and I called Jim Rome that morning. "Hud, welcome to the 'The Jungle.' What's up?"

"I just wanted to spread the news that there's a new Hud in town. I just had my first baby boy."

Rome asked, "How's he look?"

"He's great! He's right here next to me and let me tell you, he's hung like a mule."

This was after the doctors had told us that he was a healthy, baby boy. I was a proud dad but I probably shouldn't have said that about his "being hung like a mule." That was pretty much over the top. It wasn't until later in 1997, in Delta Sky magazine, with my picture on the cover in my Phillies uniform, that I first told the story about Cade having Down syndrome.

In the spring of 1997, the Phillies were opening up the season in Los Angeles to play the Dodgers. Rome called and asked me if I wanted to come into the studio to talk about Cade. It was a great interview because it gave me a chance to tell the story of what it was like to confront the news about having a child born with Down syndrome and what Jennifer and I had to go through.

When I got to the ballpark later that day the fans were running down to the dugout telling me they had heard the story on the Rome show. They were saying, "God bless you." Love started pouring down on me because I opened up my personal life to the world.

Even now the listeners of "The Jungle" always ask me how Cade is doing. The storytelling on the Rome show brought attention to our organization inspired by Cade, Team Up For Down Syndrome. I'm really grateful to Jim for that opportunity and for his sensitivity regarding my family.

Romey was a vessel for me to share my life with people. He gave me a platform to start a second career as a broadcaster. I was well spoken—actually -- not well spoken, but outspoken—and I thank him for giving me that platform.

It meant so much that Jim gave me a chance to discuss some of the deepest splinters in my life. I used that opportunity to talk about the argument with Mark Langston and to share my feelings after my final game as a professional baseball player. I called him when I got out of the hospital right after my brain hemorrhage and I called him to talk about what happened in Kansas City . . .

DEEP SPLINTERS

The two darkest times in my life both demanded that I rely on my faith in Christ to somehow survive and to learn about my own imperfection. My first great challenge came in 2000, just after I celebrated my 40th birthday on a fishing trip in Texas with my uncle. After the trip I flew from Texas to Oakland to meet up with the Angels for a series with the A's.

I arrived one day ahead of the team and was relaxing in my hotel when all of a sudden I felt a headache coming on. Every time my heart would beat it would get worse. Then I got sick to my stomach and threw up in the bathroom. I'm not one to complain about pain or physical injury. During my career I never made a big deal about being hurt. But this seemed different and I was concerned. I called Jennifer and told her I had a headache and she said, "Well, so do I. Cade just wiped what was in his diaper on the TV screen." I said, "I really have a bad headache." It was quiet on the other end of the line for a second and then she said, "Rex, you're slurring your words. You might be having a stroke. Hang up and call the front desk and get some help!"

I called the front desk and asked them to send a doctor up to the room immediately because I knew I was about to pass out. The EMT guys came up about two minutes later and I told them, "Everything is okay, I just have a bad headache."

I didn't know it but my brain was bleeding.

They wheeled me out of the room on a gurney and rushed me downstairs to an ambulance to take me to the hospital. As they were wheeling me into the ambulance, I could see a boy with Down syndrome looking back at me from the double doors to the ambulance. I was fully conscious, though I was in a lot of pain. The boy, probably about nine or 10, started climbing into the ambulance with me! The EMT told him he couldn't come with us to the hospital and the boy said, "He's going to be all right. He'll be okay. I just know he's going to be fine."

And in this dream-like state I'm thinking, "If this is not an angel from heaven, then I don't know if there will ever be one." As soon as that kid said I'd be okay, I started to believe that I was going to make it through this.

I got to the hospital and they put a needle in my spine and drew a lot of blood out. That's when the doctors knew I had a brain hemorrhage, which is a leak from a blood vessel. Every time my heart beat, it would send a pulsating pain to my brain, causing a throbbing headache. The doctor informed me that I had a serious injury and had two options for surgery to relieve the pressure in my brain.

While I was on my way to the hospital, I accidentally hit the cell phone in my pocket and it dialed my home phone number without me knowing. Jennifer heard the sounds of the ambulance on the phone—I was in no shape to talk to her and I didn't even know I'd called her. Jennifer flew to Oakland and met my broadcast partner, Steve Physioc, after she spoke with Dr. Lou Yokum, the Angels' doctor. Dr. Yokum told her to transfer me to the Stanford Medical Center before anyone did anything to my brain.

Phys picked Jennifer up at the airport. She was eight months pregnant with our third child, William, and Phys was really worried about her condition because she had been on bed rest. But the first thing she did was start cracking jokes! When they met me at the hospital, I let her know that the doctor at the Oakland hospital wanted to do surgery on me and she said, "No one is cutting on your brain! I'm worried about what might come out—a baseball, an old watch, or something." At the worst of times she continued to joke around and that let me know she felt confident that I was going to recover.

The game plan was to fly me to Stanford to get an assessment from Dr. Gary Steinberg, a leading expert on head injuries and brain trauma. They couldn't get me air-lifted until the next morning. The alternative was taking an ambulance but I was afraid I'd never make it.

The next morning three guys dressed in blue suits came into my hospital room. "Mr. Hudler, we are here to take you to Stanford."

Now I was sure I was dreaming. I had made it through a long night and I hardly slept because the pain was so intense.

As they were wheeling me to the helicopter, I asked the pilot if he could fly over Oakland-Alameda County Coliseum so that I could get a glimpse of the field where the Angels and the A's were playing. "Sir," he said, "you've had a serious injury. We're going to take you directly to the hospital. We don't have time for fly-bys."

They air-lifted me to Stanford and ran the same tests to see what was going on with my brain. When I arrived the nurse gave me a shot of something and it made the headache go away. "What did you give me?"

"We gave you a shot of Demerol."

"They were giving me morphine at the other hospital."

"You don't give brain hemorrhage patients morphine!"

Thank God I was transferred to Stanford!

My family supported me during this difficult time. My mom, her husband, Dan, and my older brother, Richard, Marlyn and his wife, Janis, came to Oakland to be with me. I had a four-day growth of beard dating back to my fishing trip and so when they saw me in the ICU, they thought I looked terrible. They went out for lunch. In the meantime, I got out of bed, looked around at the other sick people and told the nurse, "Hey, you need to give my bed to somebody who is actually sick! Where's your shower?" I cleaned up and got back into bed. My family came back from lunch and I was clean-shaven with my hair combed and they gasped—I looked healed!

The doctor came to visit me later and said, "You had a

brain hemorrhage and there was a significant amount of blood. However, we just did another brain scan and the blood is gone. The blood has evaporated and we can't explain why." We knew why! Our prayers had been answered!

Dr. Steinberg is one of the best neurosurgeons in the world. He had treated Joe Montana and Steve Young after their concussions. Now he was telling me I didn't need surgery. I'd put my life in God's hands and God was telling me it was not my time to die.

The new plan was to stay at the hospital for observation, and if everything checked out okay, I'd be cleared to go home in a few days. Of course, I felt like I was ready to go back to work right away but I was facing six weeks of rest, more tests after that, and then I could go back to broadcasting full time.

I was feeling well enough to check my voicemail and I must have had at least 40 messages! I decided to return a call to my good friend Bruce Hornsby, a great musician. I was talking to Bruce, getting all excited about feeling so good, and all of a sudden I got nauseous and threw up again. I told him not to take it personally.

After that one incident, I didn't have any more symptoms of the brain hemorrhage. I rested for another day and did a radio show from my hospital bed with Scott Kaplan and Billy Ray on the old "Mighty 1090" in San Diego.

I finally went home and the goal was to just relax, but that's easier said than done. It seemed like I'd only been home a few minutes when my son Cade began running water in the tub in the upstairs bathroom and it overflowed, causing a flood in the downstairs bathroom. Jennifer handled it for me; she told me to go into the other room and relax. I'm really blessed that I have a friend who knows how to take care of me.

Six weeks later I returned to Stanford, and they cleared me to go back to work. The doctor was very optimistic, "Son, the only thing I can tell you and your family is that less than 1% of these hemorrhages ever recur." That good news really gave me some peace of mind.

In my first game back with the Angels, they flashed my photo up on the scoreboard and I received a standing ovation. The Goodyear blimp was flying over "The Big A" and it said, "Welcome back, Hud!" It was so sweet. This was one of those moments in life when you realize the impact you have on other people when you show them love. I needed that love coming back to me after those six tough weeks. The Angels PR people brought me a huge stack of e-mail messages from fans and friends who were praying for me to get well.

I woke up every morning with Bible hymns on my heart, singing songs from my old church in Fresno. I was uplifted by the outpouring of love from so many people. The Holy Spirit was strong in me and fueled by the power of prayer.

Diane Pucin, a columnist for the *Los Angeles Times*, was also very interested. She called me after this ordeal and wrote a column about my brain hemorrhage and the little boy who appeared when they were putting me into the ambulance. She knew my son, Cade, had "Up syndrome". Pucin's article and interest in the connection between the little boy and our lives was a reaffirmation that we continue to help families that are affected by Down syndrome.

You know, I just could not get that boy from the ambulance in Oakland out of my mind for several years. He was all alone that day and that's very unusual for a child with Down syndrome. I thought that maybe he was a dream – you know, not a real person, maybe a real angel. I had to find out!

I began my search by calling the hospital to ask for the name of the ambulance service. A call to the ambulance service eventually put me in touch with the EMT and driver. The lady who drove the ambulance confirmed that the little boy was not a dream and really was there that day.

Three years after my brain hemorrhage, I was staying at the Hilton Hotel again. I was on the team bus which was just pulling away and I looked out the window and saw a boy with Down syndrome! I yelled at the bus driver to stop! "STOP the bus." I jumped off and asked the boy where his father or mother was. His dad was right there and knew me. He said, "Hey, Rex Hudler. We're big Angels fans and come to stay at this hotel when the Angels are in town." I told him that I had a brain hemorrhage a few years ago and there was a boy with Down syndrome who got on the ambulance with me. "Was it your son?" He said, "Hud, my boy is really interested in ambulances and fire engines and on the morning of your illness he ran down to the ambulance all by himself." I gave his dad TV booth passes and we got to know each other and spent some time talking and hanging out.

That was him! I found him! All that time I thought he was a dream but I finally found my angel. I believe that God knew a boy with Down syndrome would comfort me. I finally got to meet the "special" boy I had thought was an angel! You know, even though he is a real human being, I still think of him as an angel sent from God.

*****

The second deep splinter in my life was when I was arrested at the Kansas City airport. It was the stupidest thing I've ever done and something that brought a lot of pain and embarrassment to me and my family. I hope that by telling this story it will send a message to others to not make the same mistakes.

Back in 2003 I had a lot of time off during the baseball season since I wasn't broadcasting a lot of games. I flew to Kansas City with the Angels and had three days off after working the first game of a four-game series. I had a buddy who had a cabin on a lake and the two of us had just hung out and gone fishing. Foolishly, we had a small amount of grass on the trip and I believed nothing was left when I packed my bag for the flight home. I was carrying the small, wooden box -- empty as far as I knew.

A woman at security was going through every little thing

in my checked luggage and pulled out the box and handed it to her supervisor. My heart dropped. I was led down a hallway to another room and a police officer asked me to show him how to open the box. It was empty but the police officer turned it over, tapped it on the table and a few crumbs came out. He put the crumbs in a chemical solution inside a bag and it turned a color to indicate that it was marijuana.

He put me in handcuffs and I knew I was in big trouble. I had never felt so low in my life. I had to call Jennifer to tell her why I missed my flight. When I finally got to call home, I couldn't imagine what I was going to tell her. She didn't give me a chance to say much and hung up on me!

I tried to get in touch with Tim Mead, the public relations director of the Angels at that time, but since it was a Sunday, I had no way to track him down to tell him what happened.

I flew home on Monday and Jennifer asked me if I'd spoken with Tim. I told her I hadn't been able to reach him yet. The natural, human feeling is that it will all go away and no one will ever find out. I was nervous for a week until I got a call from my boss at Channel 9 in Los Angeles. "Hud, did something happen in Kansas City?"

"Yeah, what's going on?"

"We just read about the arrest on the wire and we have to release the news."

I called Tim Mead and told him what happened. Tim is a straight-up guy. He simply said that the Angels would hire another broadcaster to replace me until the matter was resolved. A short time later the Kansas City District Attorney dropped all the charges and asked me to do community service and seek counseling.

But for weeks, I was the subject of talk shows, false rumors, and it was a very humbling time. I had to tell my daughter, "Honey, with all the decisions you make in life there are consequences. I just want you to know that I made a bad decision and I was wrong. If anyone says anything about this to you, just tell them I made a mistake and I'm sorry." That was so tough! But Alyssa said, "Its okay, Daddy—I still love you!"

Arn called the Angels to see if I could get my job back and they told him I was suspended for the remainder of the 2003 season. I knew that my job with the Angels was in jeopardy.

Now, the 2003-2004 off-season came around and it brought one challenge after another. My mom's husband, Dan, died. My grandma passed away. A lot of tragedy marked one of the lowest periods in my life.

Jennifer and I had just gone to the funeral for Dan and we were in the car on the way to the cemetery for the burial. I checked my cell phone messages and I'd heard from Tim Mead. He said that the Angels had made a decision about me and I should call him immediately. I remember telling Jennifer, "What a day to find out I've lost my job. It can't get any worse."

I called Tim back and he put me on with Dennis Kuhl, the newly-hired Angels President. Dennis didn't pull any punches. "Rex, we're going to move forward this year with you as our broadcaster. We love your enthusiasm. You have what it takes to help us be a success. We want to let go of what happened in the past. You've got your job back." Jennifer and I cried. It was unreal! I got my job back! Thank you, God!

I found out later that there was an overflowing of love and letters from the Angels Booster Club and so many other fans that wanted me back in the TV booth. Once again, it's my belief that if you give love, you get love back. I'm so thankful for all the Angels fans.

During that spring training camp I was in Tempe, Arizona for a Cactus League game and as I was walking across the field during BP, the crowd started cheering. The applause kept getting louder and louder. I started looking around to see if a Hall of Fame player was down on the field, but they were cheering for me! It was overwhelming. All the pain I'd been feeling just melted away and tears came to my eyes as the fans welcomed me back.

We live in a forgiving society. I believe I was forgiven because I told everyone the truth. I was wrong and I made a bad decision. I asked for forgiveness and God told me to stand in the light. I had to be man enough to take the heat and move on with my life.

I know that I would not have gotten my job back if

public opinion had turned against me. The Angels front office kept all the letters of support I got during this time—and there were a LOT of letters. The whole experience was very humbling, especially given the relationship I had with my church and my faith in Christ.

I called Jim Rome during spring training—I was so excited to be back on the job. "There's no one out on the field yet. The grass is beautiful. It's a virgin field with no marks in the dirt on the infield. The grass smells so good."

Jim Rome said, "Wait Hud, what do you mean the grass smells so good?"

I could finally laugh about the whole thing. That's when I knew I was back, the scar was still there, but this splinter was gone.

FAMILY FIRST

Jennifer and I always wanted a large family, so no matter where we played or what city we lived in, we always tried to put our family first. When we decided to have a third child, we didn't concern ourselves with the potential of raising another child with a disability. If God wanted us to have another child with "Up Syndrome", then we would be okay with it. We believe "if God brings us to it, He will bring us through it". The odds of having another child with Up syndrome stayed the same (about 300 to 1).

William Harrison Hudler, our third child, was named William for my grandfather and Harrison in memory of Jennifer's father. William burst on the scene quickly and has not slowed down since. He was a good baby, perhaps a little ornery, but a blessing. I carried William around in a baby pouch on my chest no matter what I was doing; cooking , cleaning, yard work, etc.

William is like me; he's energetic, athletic, aggressive, confident, impatient, strong-willed, and, as his first grade teacher said, charming! (Fortunately, we only have one child like me!) His first word was "ball" and I promise I didn't teach it to him. It doesn't matter what kind of ball it is, basketball, football, soccer, tennis or baseball; if a ball is involved, he wants to play! I just love to watch his "all or nothing" style and occasionally my schedule allows me to coach some too.

When William was 16 months old, Jennifer was taking a partial birth control pill because she was nursing. She started to feel like she was pregnant. She went to the drugstore and bought a home pregnancy test and the next morning she gave me the news that it was definite—she was pregnant again! It was kind of a shock at first but I was thrilled. Three is a crowd, but one more—what the heck! We always wanted a large family!

Three months after the Angels won the 2002 World Series, Dr. Marc Winter delivered our third son. I told Jennifer that I wanted our baby to have a special name. Naming a child is very important and we wrestled with the decision. We liked David and Scott and they were the middle names of Jennifer's two brothers. Could we combine the names and use them both?

I had also heard Phys make the play by play call, "David Eckstein (the Angels' shortstop) to Scott Spezio" (the Angels' first baseman) the whole year. It had such a nice ring to it, a great combination. Scott Spezio hit the most important home run in the history of the Angels' franchise. He hit the key three-run homer to bring us back from the brink of disaster in Game 6 of the 2002 World Series. "Honey, David Eckstein is one of my heroes. He's become a great baseball player with the skills he's been given; a little giant and a World Champion. That's it! Yes, David Scott Hudler!"

SPLINTERS

David Scott Hudler has the perfect baseball name. Although he plays ball and is my only left-handed batter, he would much rather sit quietly and play with Legos or puzzles. He loves to read and color, so he was thrilled to finally get to go to school like his brothers and sister. He's very sweet natured and caring and he's very sharp. Nothing gets by David. He always knows where everyone in the family is and what they need.

So, the Hudler family is complete. There are nine years between my eldest child, Alyssa, and my youngest child, David. I'm bound to get a dose of what my mom went through in raising three boys, but I always welcome a challenge. Bring it on! Let's have some fun with it.

When I am on the road doing baseball games, my children can watch me on TV. When I'm holding my microphone at the top of the broadcast and Steve Physioc says, "And this is Rex Hudler," I raise my pinkie finger as a secret signal to tell them that I love them and that I'm thinking about them. How many kids can see their dad on TV when he goes away on a business trip? I always try to look at the positive side of traveling during the baseball season.

I have this positive attitude because of my faith in Jesus Christ. My favorite Bible verse as a young ballplayer was James 1:1 "Consider it pure joy my brothers, when we face trials of many kinds. The testing of our faith will develop patience and perseverance that we may not be lacking in anything". God teaches that our faith will develop patience and perseverance.

That verse has helped me to become a better parent while working away from home for six months and then having six months at home. When I'm gone for long stretches over the baseball season, there's potential for conflicts with Jennifer about how to deal with the kids when I come home. Here's what I've been doing lately to remedy that—I back off or at least I try! I come home and ease in. I don't say a word which is hard for me.

I believe this is sound advice for any father or mother who travels for their jobs. We need to see how it's been running without us and respect that routine. Jennifer has it under control in the Hudler family. She's managing the house, the school schedule and paying the bills. She also finds time to teach music, volunteer in the kids' classrooms and run "Team Up". My first instinct is to start changing the established daily routines but I know better than to shake things up too much the minute I come home. It always takes about a month or so to adjust.

Cooking is one of the ways I ease into the family routine as a stay-at-home dad in the off-season. My mom always cooked meals for me and my two brothers. My grandma and great-grandma were also really good, southern cooks and good food was a big part of growing up for me. I watched my mom prepare those home-cooked meals and I picked up a few things. For instance, my brothers and I used to make donuts out of canned biscuits. We'd fry up the dough, shake up the little donut holes in a bag of powdered sugar, and we had the best donuts in the world! I'd never let my kids take a chance of getting burned now but back then it didn't seem like a big deal to fry up that dough in hot oil.

One of our favorite breakfasts is the "Marlyn Specialty" named for my dad. It's a piece of buttered toast with the middle taken out, grilled with an egg in the hole, cooked on both sides for three minutes. Now I'm cooking the "Marlyn Specialty" at home for my kids and they love it with bacon. I get up in the morning and I become a short-order cook.

With four kids I have to spread myself around and some days there's just not enough of me. It's hard to be a good father. Anyone can be a dad, but to be a good dad—wow, you have to take it to a different level. For one thing, I decided to forget about playing golf very often. I need to spend time at home with my kids and make a positive impact on my family. If you want to instill qualities of good character in your kids you will need to spend time with them. Your children are with you for such a short time. Don't waste it! Don't miss any of their formative years!

I remember teaching Alyssa how to ride a bike on a hill at the park. Now, she's in high school and playing at the park days with her are already over! She's 14 and what I've found is that consistent love is important. With her I really learned, as Jennifer said, that my tone of voice could be hurtful. Coming from a family of all boys, I had to learn from experience that girls are different. I could see the hurt in her eyes if I raised my voice. I have to remember that I'm speaking to my sweet, young daughter, not to another ball player. Now, I enjoy supporting her and watching her sing, act, and play sports. She's a beautiful, young lady.

Cade is twelve now! I can't believe it - - where does the time go? He's riding horses, snow skiing and playing on the Challenger Little League team. But, we're most proud that he's reading and writing and speaking more clearly. He's brought perspective to all of our lives, including grandmas and grandpas. He has unbridled joy and unconditional love for everyone!

William has a great sense of humor and a big heart. He prefers watching *Feed the Children* outreach programs to cartoons on Sunday morning TV. He told me, "Daddy, I feel sorry for those kids. Can we take some of our cereal and send it to them?" I told him that we should call and pledge money, so we did. All the *Feed the Children* mail comes in the name of William Hudler. He's proud of helping other children in need and is inspired to support other kids less fortunate. William has compassion!

We all pray together as a family because I believe that if we pray together, we stay together. All of their individual prayers are so sweet, but David's prayers are detailed for his age. He prays specifically for family members like Annie-Grannie, Maw-Maw Peggy, and Grandma Kathy as they've had health issues. David has a very loving heart.

I want my kids, when they are older, to be able to say, "My daddy loved me! He was there for me. He cooked. We went to the park. We went to the golfing range. He came to my school plays. We had fun together." We have so little time to enjoy being with our kids before they grow up and leave home. I want them to remember me as a dad who loved them. Love is the greatest thing that God commands from us. I love people! I want to instill that character in my children. I want to teach them that God says in the Scripture, "People will know you are a Christian by the way you love other people."

It's important as a father for me to teach my kids manners, to teach them to be polite and to respect adults. I grew up saying "yes, sir" and that's what impressed George Steinbrenner the first time I met him at Yankee Stadium. My parents were always praised by other parents because we were such polite kids. I would hear those comments and it made me feel good. I want my kids to be polite and respectful too.

I'm still learning through my wife how to be a good dad. Instead of yelling from across the room like I used to, Jennifer asks me to get up and go talk to my kids. My tone of voice can be too harsh at times and she'll tell me, "Be a little gentler; this is not the ball field. These are your tender children."

For example, I took Alyssa to play softball when she was eight years old and this was the first time I got to see any of my children compete in sports. She hit a one-hopper back to the pitcher, ran halfway to first base and peeled off and went into the dugout. She didn't even run to the bag. I was standing down the first-base line with my Aunt Mina McCutcheon and I freaked! My mouth fell open!! Alyssa was only the tender age of eight, but I started after her and Aunt Mina grabbed me by my shirt and yanked me back. "Hey, back off! Take it easy. What are you doing? She's a little girl. If you tell her something critical now, it's going to crush her—talk to her later."

That was the perfect advice. Mina was right. Alyssa was not playing major league baseball. But I was thinking, "She's a Hudler and a Hudler has to hustle. Her dad made a living from hustling!" But thankfully, Aunt Mina was there to restrain me from saying the wrong thing. I believe God puts people in our lives to help us to do the right thing. Aunt Mina has been a great support for us, especially Alyssa.

On the way home from the game, after I'd calmed down, I told Alyssa, "In baseball—even if they catch the ball—you always run through the base. Pretend that you haven't eaten for a week and there's food on the other side of first base." I broke it down in a way that I thought would make sense to her. I was very gentle. I've learned that's the approach that children need.

I know my kids love me when I come home from a road trip and they come running to me. Cade yells, "Daddy's home," and he watches as I greet each of my kids in unique and special ways. With the little boys it is "Up in the sky, Daddy" and I throw 'em up and it's like they're flying and then I catch 'em. Cade is so big now that I can barely get him up in the sky, but I still try.

I love to tell the kids bedtime stories almost every night when I'm home, or I read to them. "Daddy, tell us a story!" I make up stories about two boys because my youngest boys, David and William, bunk together. I'll lie down on the floor and use my imagination and it's so much fun. David, my youngest boy, will say, "Daddy, no scary stories!" Then William will say, "Come on Dad, give us a scary story."

We always close the story time with a prayer, "God, thank you for loving us and thank you for my boys. I pray that you'll help me be a good daddy and that you'll help me to have patience with them. Help them to understand that it's important to obey their parents and help me to understand that it's important for me to love my kids. Lord, help them to be kind to other kids at school and help them to be gentle. Let them understand, Lord, that's it is okay to not be first—it's okay to be second or third. It's okay to be last sometimes. God bless all of our family and friends." Then I'll give them a kiss goodnight.

I hear other parents say that time is so short and the kids will be gone and out of the house before we know it. I want to let my children know that I loved being a part of their lives while they were growing up.

ATTITUDE AND OUTPUT

Life is not just a given—it's an opportunity. We can make decisions about how we are going to live our lives, what we are going to do, the process it takes, and the commitment we have to make to be a good person.

I am knee deep in family right now, one of the greatest commitments of all. I shuttle the children, I shovel food in their little, hungry mouths, I share at their schools and work noon playground duty. I read, I bathe, I wrestle and cuddle. There's "up in the sky, Daddy" and "let's play ball. Take me to the park, the movies, to Disneyland and the zoo too, today!" It brings me joy now to sit on the bench and watch my children playing their games.

I am so blessed to have four children that fill my life with so many things; with love, joy, peace(?), goodness, laughter and tears. They lift my spirits and help me to realize what's important in my life. In considering the fruits of the spirit, it's not always peaceful, my patience is tried, and we're not always kind to each other. Gentleness . . . . well, with three boys and a strong, athletic girl . . . . I try to show my faithfulness consistently to my children, but it doesn't always show. I know God continues to refine my self-control.

Jennifer helps me and together we make a good team.

We lift each other up when the other's down. We strike a good balance in the raising of our family. I am so thankful for my wife. She's such a loving and supportive wife and understands my splinters.

Splinters can go deep but most are just below the surface. The deeper the splinter, the longer it takes for the wound to heal. Deep ones need more attention and time. I believe we can learn from a splinter that goes deeper, although it's more painful.

My family means everything to me. From my very first family until now, I've learned so much. My mother and fathers and step-parents were the examples and I've learned a lot from them. I take from them the good and apply it to my life today. I realize it's not always easy to be a good father. I've been disappointed in my life and I don't want to disappoint, but I do from time to time. I take the splinters out, I learn what I can from those experiences and I try to be better. I refuse to let negative thoughts or influences guide me because I know God truly has us in the palm of his hand.

My commitment to my family has a lot to do with the fact that I came from a broken home. I had plenty of attention from my mom and then from Marlyn, but Jack didn't always fulfill my needs as a father.

Jack's drinking was a splinter in our lives that was removed when he stopped drinking and turned his life around. We then had a great relationship and he and my mom became friends later in life too. He was a real pillar in his church and community. He and his wife, Kathy, loved us and our children. Kathy is still a wonderful Grandma whom we love very much. Sadly, we lost Jack in 2002 but we are comforted by Romans 8:28 that says, "And we know that all things work together for good to those who love God, to those who are called according to His purpose."

What began as a big splinter that tore our family apart, has evolved into a huge, happy extended family. Today my children are blessed to have my mom, Annie, Grandma Kathy, Grandpa Hud (Marlyn) and Nana Janis, Great-Grandma Mobley, Jennifer's mom, Maw Maw Peggy and her husband, Paw Paw Ken. Although we have lived in 7 cities and 3 countries, family has always come first. No matter where God has placed us on this earth, we have made it a priority to visit them and they have visited us as often as possible. Our children are blessed to have so many loving people in their lives.

My Heavenly Father wants what is best for me and so I continue to be positive about my life experiences everyday and say, "Thank you God for who I am today, where I've been and how you've continued to teach me through it all." Joshua 24:15 sums it up for me . . . . "As for me and my house, we will serve the Lord." He is our strength through all life's circumstances.

What about the splinters in your life? Have you tried to get them out or are you letting them fester and take you down? When you feel overwhelmed, shake yourself! Don't be afraid to go to your family, friends, pastor, mentor, your Bible, prayer and God. Get past the pain; pull 'em out! Deal with them! Don't dwell on the negative; focus on the positive. Don't sit still and don't give up! You'll realize some of those splinters really weren't that deep. Forgive and move on. Move on so you can see how God is going to use you and your situations and how you can handle them for His good if you let Him help you. I'm sure you'll be amazed at what's in store for you.

Playing baseball was a blast and I couldn't be more thankful to still be in the game today broadcasting. I love motivating and encouraging young players too. As a baseball player and now as a broadcaster I have only two things I can control: My attitude and my "all-out" effort to perform at my very best. To be successful in any career, whether you're a ballplayer or a banker, you need an attitude that's forgiving, positive and uplifting for other people. As a player, I couldn't worry about what the weather was like, if I'd be in the lineup, or if I was on the trading block. I couldn't control those things so why worry about them? I focused on attitude and output, the only two things I could control.

So, I hope you will learn from your mistakes as I try to do. Don't stay focused on your splinters. Look to your future . . . . tomorrow is brand new day.

Remember . . . .

Be a fountain, not a drain!

ACKNOWLEDGEMENTS

I thank you, Lord, for all you've given me and the opportunities you provide to share with others.

Thank you to my family for allowing me to make mistakes while learning to be a more caring and patient father.

Thank you to my mom who believed in me and has always been my #1 fan.

Thank you to Jennifer and Judee Stapp for helping me put the stories and words where it all made sense.

Thank you to Teena Myers and Stacey Grable for your input during the crunch time.

Thank you to Adriana Macias for caring for our family and home with love.

I would like to thank my friend, Jim Rosenthal. It was fun telling my stories to you.

Thank you to those who care enough to buy this book and share my life so faithfully.

Pictured on the back cover:
The Hudler Family in a Little League dugout. (Clockwise from the left: Alyssa, Jennifer, William, David and Cade surrounding Rex.)

Photo by John Cordes

Cover Design by Q Aloi - PSB The Marketing SuperSource

Proudly printed by Don Arnold at D.M. Steele Co. Printing
Fullerton, CA